Discoverir

"This book is bursting with the kind of inspiration entrepreneurs search for, day after day. Not a mere How-to book, *Discovering Your Inner Samurai* will help you focus your energy inward — to find that inner sense of wonderment which led you to exploring the world of being an entrepreneur in the first place. After reading this book, you will hear the voice of your Inner Samurai guiding you to greater success, with confidence and self-assuredness. Read it over and over, until that still, strong voice becomes second nature to you, and you will be assured of reaching all of your goals."

Jordan Adler
Entrepreneur and Network
    Marketing Top Money Earner
Jerome, AZ
www.jordanadler.com

"Engaging! Enlightening! Empowering! In *Discovering Your Inner Samurai,* Susan L. Reid shares refreshing ideas about a variety of topics that are critical to your business success whether you are an entrepreneur by surprise or by design. Her delightful real life stories illustrate how just a slight shift in how you see yourself, your business, and your life can catapult you into a new level success that is grounded and true to who you are deep in your core."

Carol McClelland, PhD
Author of *Your Dream Career for Dummies*
    and *The Seasons of Change*
Transition Dynamics Enterprises, Inc.
Menlo Park, CA
www.transitiondynamics.com

"Business is first and foremost about people. Customers, employees, and investors are people . . . and so are you. There are thousands of books about the strategies and mechanics of business, this book is about you, the entrepreneur/business owner . . . and helping you understand you! The secret to your success is knowing who you are, and what you do with you! This book is a must read for all entrepreneurs!"

Jim Horan
Author of best-selling book series,
The One Page Business Plan (for Creative Entrepreneurs, Non-Profits, Professional Consultants, Financial Services)
Berkeley, CA
www.onepagebusinessplan.com

"Amazing, inspiring, insightful, and moving! Like a conversation with a wise and passionate friend, Susan's words will energize you to 'think outside of the box,' to listen to and trust your own inner truth, and to find courage and companionship in the journey of other women. Begin to imagine that the creation of your business will be more glorious than the expected and desired outcome and Susan will inspire you through the process!"

Robin Lipke, PhD
Clinical Psychologist
Lame Deer, MT

"I couldn't stop reading. I was drawn first by one thread of thought and then another and another as a fabric of deeper self-understanding wove itself into my beliefs and challenges as a woman, a solo-preneur and a life coach. This book is full of powerful truths, sage wisdom, effortless empowerment, and passion."

Jina Daigle MS, LPC
Consultant, Trainer and Coach
Owner and Founder of Creative Team Solutions
    and Creative Life Solutions
Dallas, TX
www.creativeteamsolutions.com

"Glorious! Susan has put together a guide to personal and professional ass-kicking (even if the ass that really needs to be kicked is your own). A power-shot of business wisdom to catapult your success!"

Andy Wibbels
Author of *Blogwild: A Guide to
    Small Business Blogging*
Chicago, IL
www.andywibbels.com

"Susan L. Reid's book beautifully displays the synthesis that Susan, the epitome of a polymath, has attained in her own life. Through the words the reader can go through the recesses of Susan's very being, and through her vulnerability we begin to expose our own, realizing the inner strength we have in that honesty. Her inner voice speaks to us, until we begin to hear our own inner voice womaning along with Susan. Although the book focuses on entrepreneurship, the reader needn't be starting a business; we can all learn the secrets of the accidental pren-her as we take stock of our working lives. Susan L. Reid has captured the following: 'Don't ask what the world needs. Ask what makes you come alive and go and do it. Because what the world needs are people who have come alive.' (attributed to Howard Thurman)"

Susan L. Wiesner, PhD
Dance Scholar and Digital Humanist
University of Virginia Library
Charlottesville, VA

"On the cutting edge! There are many books available with practical guidelines for business startups that are now incorporating emotional and psychological factors . . . Suze Orman, for instance. However, Susan's book is the cutting edge of a new paradigm of business manuals. It's the first business book I've seen to incorporate the spiritual along with the practical, emotional, and mental factors. It's *The Secret* for business."

Muzetta Swann
Founder and President of Willow Oak
    Center for Arts & Learning
    at Robertson County
Springfield, TN
www.willowoakarts.org

"*Discovering Your Inner Samurai* is at once informative, wise, inspirational, engagingly readable, and filled with warm humor. This book offers a road map to harnessing the power of your inner wisdom as the key to realizing your most treasured dreams and, like Dorothy traveling the yellow brick road to Oz, you discover that whatever you are seeking 'over the rainbow' is always 'in your own back yard.' What a comforting message."

Max Wellspring
Author of the soon to be released,
    Love Your Body, Love Your Life,
    The Power of Trust, The Receiving
    Journal . . . Activating The Universal
    Law of Allowing e-Books and
    Heart Health Meditations CD
Life and Business Coach
Certified Prosperity Partnership Guide
    and Emotional Freedom Facilitator
The Wellspring Solution
Los Angeles, CA
www.thewellspringsolution.com

"Relevant and empowering for those beyond the Accidental Preneur! *Discovering your Inner Samurai* is a book that challenges and empowers women to be their authentic selves. Whether you are an entrepreneur or not, this book will resonates with anyone searching for their personal identity and desiring to connect to their Inner Samurai!"

Sonya Gabrielle Baker, DM
Associate Professor of Music
   and Professional Singer
Murray, KY
www.sonyabaker.com

Discovering Your Inner Samurai

The Entrepreneurial Woman's
Journey to Business Success

Dr. Susan L. Reid

Discovering Your Inner Samurai: The Entrepreneurial Woman's Guide to Business Success

Copyright © 2007 by Susan L. Reid, DMA
All rights reserved. Printed in USA.

ISBN-10: 1-934229-05-9
ISBN-13: 978-1-934229-05-7

Editor: Yvonne DiVita
Cover Design: Karin Marlett Choi
Page Layout/Design: Karin Marlett Choi
Cover illustration: Dana Weekley of www.ninetomatoes.com
   Copyright © 2007 by Dana Weekley

Published by:
   WME Books
   Windsor Media Enterprises, LLC
   Rochester, New York, USA

TrueType Font *Orient2*, used courtesy of **FreeFonts.com**

Available online at: **www.WMEBooks.com**, as well as other booksellers and distributors worldwide.

Special Sales:
This and other WME Books titles are available at special discounts for bulk purchases, for use in sales promotions, or as premiums. Special editions, including personalized covers, excerpts of existing books, and corporate imprints, can be created in large quantities for special needs or projects.

For more information, please contact:
   Special Book Orders
   Windsor Media Enterprises, LLC
   282 Ballad Avenue
   Rochester, NY 14626
   1-877-947-BOOK (2665)
   info@wmebooks.com

This book is dedicated in loving memory to my parents:

Jane S. Reid
Roseann B. Reid
L. Leon Reid

Amor aeternum

ACKNOWLEDGEMENTS

Writing this book has been a labor of love, made all the more delightful by those who shared the journey with me. Many thanks to Andy Wibbels who provided the platform for a dozen or so aspiring authors to come together and write most intently, intensely, and ardently over a 45-day period.

Thank you to Verna Wilder, my first book editor, who told me the truth and to my current editor, Mary Ellen Whitaker, who made my text pop.

The folks at WME Books have been outstanding. I am so appreciative of Yvonne DiVita, my publisher and developing editor who believed in me, in my book, and most importantly, gave me the space to write — you are my messenger of Guan. I am grateful to Karin Marlett Choi for her inner inspired cover design and to Tom Collins and Karin for their page layout and design.

I've been blessed with a wonderful group of friends who supported me in fabulous ways during the writing of this book. To Jina Daigle and Linda Childs, who believe in the power of personal stories; to Robin Lipke for her expert psychological advice throughout this book; to Linda Franklin for her detailed proof reading; to the Ah-Ha Sisterhood whose spirit carried me forward.

Thank you to my colleagues, Carolyn Freeman for her fine-toothed proof reading of this book, to Carol McClelland who brainstormed with me and offered her been-there-done-that author perspective.

To Jordan Adler who walks the talk, to Jim Horan for his Zen inspiration, and to Susan Wiesner, Muzetta Swann, Max Wellspring, Sonya Baker, and BZ Riger for their reading. Special thanks to Susan Olson for her written-from-the- heart preface, and for giving me my first Abe tape.

Special thanks to the hundreds of clients who have shared their entrepreneurial journey with me. Your courage, conviction, and willingness to know your inner self, your Inner Samurai, formed the cornerstone of many of the ideas for this book. Your personal and business success greatly inspired me. Particular thanks to Dana Weekley for hearing the call and saying "yes."

Finally, to my brother Larry for his attention to historical accuracy, and for knowing that *even Samurai need teddy bears.*

Table of Contents

	Foreword	xi
	Preface	xv
	Introduction	1
Part I	**Dealing With Change**	
1	And So I Begin . . .	9
2	Now What?	31
3	The Shift	45
4	Tao	57
Part II	**The Accidental Pren-her Way**	
5	Doing What You Love Multiple Streams of Passion	71
6	The Hero's Journey A Heroine's Approach	95
7	The Strength of Intuition	117
Part III	**Discovering Your Inner Samurai**	
8	What in The Heck is Resistance? Effortless Action and the Inner Samurai	141
9	The Art of Goal Setting	159
10	Scapegoats Extraordinaire: Time and Money	185
11	Connect To Give, Not Connect to Get	207
12	Home Alone: The Difference Between Isolation and Solitude	227
13	Scheduling Chaos	247
14	The Secret to Your Business Success	263
	Resources	275
	A Note from the Illustrator	277
	Notes	279
	Index	283

Foreword

Get ready for the cheese to move — smell the cheese often so you know when it is getting old.

—Spencer Johnson, MD

How many cares one loses when one decides not to be something, but to be someone.

—Coco Chanel

You're going to love this book — I did! I have known Susan nearly 20 years and, as a friend and avid choral music lover, have joyfully connected with the wonderful personal and professional journey of this talented, intelligent, innovative, competent, funny, open-minded, caring, often "out of the box," and lovely spirit.

Susan is known as a loyal friend; you can trust her. This book is Susan; you can trust it. You will likely want to keep it by your bedside — and in your office. It will lead you with essential truths that pull you forward while winding back through your own unique self, your Inner Samurai, as Susan names it, happily teaching you to feel safe in its guidance.

Discovering Your Inner Samurai will encourage and excite you, while keeping you focused and grounded. She will tell you her story, always with that touch of "Susan humor," and the inspiring stories of those she has helped; she will ask you questions about yourself, the answers to which she already knows because she's been there, done that, and moved on.

Through my profession as a psychologist, I've seen women struggle with fears and doubts that have kept them from exploring their potentials and living their dreams. In this complicated era of information overload and high expectations, women often feel confused and overwhelmed attempting to spin too many plates on too many poles, coping but not really living. They need encouragement and simplicity to see through the fog.

You may be one of these women, a woman who wants to fulfill that entrepreneur dream whether it is big or small, and do it effortlessly. Look no further; I urge you to begin here with *Discovering Your Inner Samurai*. It is an important book whose yoke is light. The secrets of *The Secret* are available for you as Susan teaches you how to give your dream the clarity of being both grand and specific. Susan takes the fear out, takes the "shoulds" and "shouldn'ts" out. She knows you are "The Little Engine That Could" and how to help you gain the confidence to create your "can-do." And she does it in the best and highest way — from the inside out.

How delicious to find that you can learn to think your passion into success and simply "know" the next logical step — always. You can even reframe the "dreaded" networking and sales into fun ways

Foreword

of connecting. You are a woman; Susan says you're already good at it.

Here you will find your dreams without confining bars; they're planted in the soil of embracing your personal freedom. You will think and feel differently. You will find change purposeful and exciting rather than frightening. You will leave resistance behind and embrace yourself and your ideas with an open heart. You will become aware.

You will live your life from another place; you will honor yourself and your journey and you will own it. You will know the presence within you and you will become acquainted with your creative spirit.

Susan is giving you this book from her own Inner Samurai; it is yours from her personal self, and it is a beautiful gift. It speaks from her knowledge, her experience, her wisdom, and her success. It points the way to yours. It's a book you will read, remember, and use happily until its pages are tattered, because it is about you recreating you, maybe many times, and lovin' it!

Susan Olson, PhD

Tacoma, WA

Preface

To see a world in a grain of sand, and heaven in a wildflower, hold infinity in the palm of your hand, and eternity in an hour.

— William Blake

The story you are about to read is my story. It's the chronicle of my journey from Accidental Pren-her™ to entrepreneurial woman.

However, I do not stand alone in its rendering; neither do I stand alone in its experience. My story is your story. Just as sure as your story is mine. In each chapter, on each page, will be stories and experiences you will recognize. On each page, in every paragraph, will be joys and sorrows that you will call your own. And within each paragraph will be words and phrases you will resonate with that you will swear you penned yourself.

This book is about discovering the Inner Samurai that all women carry deep within, at the center of our being. Our Inner Samurais are the repository of all our life experiences, alchemized from lead into pure gold. A woman's Inner Samurai is her place of absolute knowing and personal power. It is the seat of her wisdom and inner strength. It is also the place of her extraordinary uniqueness.

The journey to discovering your Inner Samurai is the connective thread that unites us all.

For Everything There Is A Season

Whenever the unexpected lands in your path, it is always a stepping-stone to where you intend to go. Train wrecks are just trains changing tracks, and there is a reason and perfection for everything.

I first came to know this when I was a young child. My mother was diagnosed with cancer when I was three-and-a-half (you know, the "and-a-half" is important at that age). I remember exactly when I knew this, though I'm not sure I was actually ever told. I see it in my three-and-a-half-year-old eyes every time I look at a particular photo taken by my dad. It's of my Grandmother Stewart, my mom and me. We were in Cape May, New Jersey — a place we often went on vacation. My grandmother is wearing a stylish dark blue hat with the mesh visor tucked carefully into the fold. She is standing slightly behind and to the left of my mother. My mom has on a fashionable short-sleeved dress, her long arms resting lightly on the boardwalk railing, her fingers casually intertwined. I am on my mom's left in front of my grandmother. I am wearing black patent-leather shoes with white lace anklets and a dress with delicate purple flowers on it and a wide purple sash. I am gripping the second railing, lower down, with both hands.

What unites us is the look on our faces. We are all dour. Not one of us is smiling. My three-and-a-half-year-old eyes look serious. It's as if a great knowing was in them. Every time I look at that picture, the same involuntary expression comes to mind, and I think to myself, "You knew, didn't you?" Yes, I did know, and my mom getting sicker and sicker as the cancer spread throughout her lymph system confirmed my knowing. This was my first brush with unexpected occurrences.

We had a housekeeper during that time, Mrs. McMillan. She lived with us during the week and went home on weekends. As my mom's health declined, Mrs. McMillan began taking care of me more and more. While my dad was at work, Mrs. McMillan and I would fold clothes, read stories, and do nice things for my mom together. One day, we were outside scouting in our autumn flower garden for some blue hydrangeas. I was quite set about picking blue hydrangeas for my mom's bedside table because that was my mother's favorite flower.

Of course, being so late in the season, the blue hydrangeas by the side of the house were all gone. Undaunted, I made us search all the flower beds for blooming blue hydrangeas, telling Mrs. McMillan, "I'm sure there is one alive somewhere!" We could not find even one, and I could not be persuaded to substitute the rich yellow and maroon hardy mums for the blue hydrangeas. That's when Mrs. McMillan turned to me and said, "You know, Susan, there is a time and season for everything." I stopped, dead in my tracks, looking angrily up at her. She lovingly held my gaze. She looked sad. I felt my throat tighten with tears. I slowly unfolded my hand, releasing the few dried hydrangeas I'd been able to find. I said, "I know." Then the child who was soon to experience the first major loss of her life quickly turned and ran to the house, into her mother's arms, sobbing.

My mom died a couple weeks later. At her funeral, I heard, for the first time, the scripture verse associated with Mrs. McMillan's words. "To everything there is a season, a time for every purpose under the sun. A time to be born and a time to die; a time to plant and a time to pluck up that which is planted,"[1] and on it goes. From those words sprung great knowing in my young five-year-old heart — as well as in my old soul.

Dear God

It took me a long time to cope with the loss of my mother. It took me even longer to gain perspective and insight about her death. Within a year after my mom's passing, my dad remarried. His new wife was someone I grew to love and who loved me fully as her daughter. Still, I suffered from self-worth and abandonment issues. I was angry with God for taking my mom, and even angrier with my new mom for taking her place. There was no outlet for that anger, so I turned it inward, becoming sullen and withdrawn. Then one day when I was seven, while doing homework at my desk in my playroom, I whipped out a sheet of paper and started writing a letter to God.

"Dear God," I began. "I am thankful for you sending me a new mommy but, what I really want to know is why you had to take my mom to be with you in heaven. Don't you have enough people there with you already?" I continued by extolling all of her many favorable qualities and the reasons why I needed her more than God did. I went on for two pages in careful cursive writing — I wanted God to be able to read every word I had written — and

Preface

ended with "Sincerely, Susan Lee Reid." (The Lee part was important because I wanted God to know which Susan Reid was asking). Now that the letter was finished, I didn't know what to do with it. Obviously, there was nowhere to send it. No one to give it to. Therefore, I stuffed it in my secret cubbyhole above my desk, waiting for God to find the letter.

Each day when I did my homework, I would take out that letter and look at it. Sometimes I would erase a word, add a word, and change a phrase around. Soon, my letter became quite smudged and hard to read. So, I wrote another one, careful to copy exactly what I had written from the first one. Now I had two letters addressed to God that were secretly squirreled away ... waiting.

Months went by, and the collection of letters had grown to six. I stopped writing in pencil at draft number four. I thought ink was more formal and professional looking. I wanted God to know that my asking was in earnest, and that I was sincere. Then, it occurred to me that God might not know where my letter was, since it was hidden away in a special place. Therefore, at the end of my prayers each night, I began tacking on a p.s.: "God, the letter that I wrote to you is downstairs above my desk in the secret drawer." Still, nothing happened.

Before long, I was leaving the secret drawer open, just a little, to make things easier for God. Don't get me wrong; I understood God to be all-powerful and all-mighty. It was just that the letter was, after all, squirreled away in a *secret hiding place*. I thought God might need a little help finding it. Six more months went by. I was coming up on my eighth birthday when I got the bright idea to put a yellow smiley face on the drawer. I let God know: "God, the letter is in the secret drawer above my desk with a yellow smiley face on it." And lo and behold . . . it finally worked! One day, I found a response, written carefully with a black fountain pen:

> Susie Q, giving birth to you was your mother's greatest joy. She was never happier than when holding you in her arms, rocking you to sleep, and watching you explore the world around you. She was very sad to leave you, though hasn't gone far away. She is near and always will be with you. You are loved, doubly much, because you now have two moms: One in heaven to watch over you like a guardian angel, and the other one to guide and nurture you here on Earth.

The collection of letters to God was gone, and in their place was this letter from my dad. Much better than any answer to the question, "Why did you have to take my mom to live with you in heaven," came the response that I was loved — doubly loved! My dad looked past the pain and hurt of a confused and still grieving child to answer the real question beneath. This unexpected response, from God's messenger, taught me a valuable lesson: It's not the answers to the questions that are important. What matters is that we allow our inner knowing to enter every situation. Ask the questions, sure! Then, be open to the real — sometimes unexpected — answers. Letting go of the need to know gives rise to something greater coming from within.

May your inner journey bring you great insight, delight, and knowing. And, when you've come to a place on your path where you can sit down, rest, and enjoy the view, write and tell me all about it. I'll be waiting to hear from you. After all, your journey and mine are one and the same.

Introduction

Begin doing what you want to do now. We have only this moment, sparkling like a star in our hand — and melting like a snowflake.

— Marie Beynon Ray

This book was a year in the writing and three years in the making. Its humble beginnings were in the spiritual awakening that I had in June of 2004, though I did not know at that time, that that event would be the catalyst for the beginning of this book. From then until now, this book and what you are about to read has survived and been enriched by the passing of both my parents, the ending of several significant relationships, the selling of my family home, the settling of two estates, three years of change, two years of grief, the starting of two businesses, a career shift, one massive re-write . . . and a partridge in a pear tree.

In short, this book has survived and been made better by the alchemical transformation that has occurred within me. As a result of both inner and outward forces that have come to bear in and on my life, I have been changed. I hope you, too, will be changed when you read about my journey and countless others from Accidental Pren-her to entrepreneurial woman.

As you read this book, it is likely that you will laugh, cry, smile, nod, and resonate with the experiences of my clients, friends, colleagues, and acquaintances (whose names and other identifying markers have been changed to honor their privacy). You might even feel angry or frustrated with some of them. In most cases, though, your heart will go out to them. You will admire their courage and reach out to support them as they face their fears.

"Mi viaje es tu viaje" are the words I use to describe this book. "Mi viaje es tu viaje" means "My journey is your journey." This is what you will come to know when you read this book. We are on this journey and in this journey together.

ACCIDENTAL PREN-HER

There are two things you need to know at the start of our journey. The first is this: The underlying philosophy of this book is that there are no accidents. *Everything that happens in your life happens for a reason, for your higher good and greater well-being, even if you don't recognize it as such at the time.* Consequently, every supposed accident is considered an "accident by design."

The second thing you need to know is that I like to make up words. For instance, I playfully add endings to existing words, such as "womaning" to explain the unique way that women get to know each other. You will also notice that I combine words to make completely new meanings.

Two terms in particular, *Accidental Pren-her* and *Inner Samurai*, are terms I have made up for this book. You won't find them anywhere else (except on my website, www.Alkamae.com, and blog, www.susanreid.typepad.com). I coined these terms because there were no other words to describe what I wanted to convey. Understanding them will make your reading all the more meaningful.

An Accidental Pren-her is a woman who finds herself starting up a business, perhaps for the very first time. She probably has had no, or very little, experience starting up a business, though she may have exhibited early entrepreneurial leanings as a child. It is most likely that she has a dream — something she has been thinking about for a very long time — although she has taken no significant action to foster that dream's development.

The "accidental" part comes in because most women, when faced with starting up a business for the very first time, say that they never anticipated doing so. They may have been happily working in corporate, academic, or other traditional workplaces for most of their adult lives until something happened. What happened? Some kind of activating event — something big enough that it required them to view life differently from that point on.

For some, they were downsized. For others, they lost their job by getting laid off or fired. Still others decided they wanted more out of life than working for a paycheck, so they quit. Sometimes the activating event was getting married, becoming a mother, or children growing up and leaving home. The loss of a parent or other loved one caused some women to rethink life. Other activating events include divorce, near fatal accidents, recovery from a serious illness, and, as was the case for me, spiritual awakenings.

Whatever the activating event, all Accidental Pren-hers share a common theme: They know that something unexpected has happened to them and that this event is now shaping who they are and what they do.

INNER SAMURAI

The next term I made up is *Inner Samurai*. This term is best defined by describing its opposite. Throughout this book, I use two phrases: *the voice inside your head* **and** *your inner voice.* These mean two very different things. The voice inside your head, for most people, is your most dominant voice, the voice that keeps up a steady chatter almost all the time. Often you are not even aware of it. Other times, it keeps you from getting any sleep. This is the voice of the mind, of the ego. It is ever focused on the past or the future. It is never focused in the present.

The opposite of that is your inner voice. Your inner voice is the voice within. Your inner voice, for most, is your secondary voice. (This book, though, will teach you ways to change that around). It is a quiet, sure voice. It is focused only in the present, and never on the past or future. Its place, power, and relevance are in the now.

Known by many names, it has been called the voice within, the inner knower, God Self, Soul,

God Within, and Spirit, to name a few. When I was younger, I used to call it "my still small voice." Then, when I was in my 30s, "the voice within." In my 40s, it became "my inner knower," and now it is "my Inner Samurai."

I began calling it my Inner Samurai when I realized how strong, vast, and powerful my inner voice is. *Inner* because the voice is deep within my being (to distinguish it from the voice inside my head) and *Samurai* because of how strong and powerful it is. Inner Samurais can move mountains, leap over tall buildings in a single bound, and stop charging wildebeests in their tracks. One of my clients calls her Inner Samurai her Inner Super Woman. I like that!

No matter what you call it, everyone has an inner voice. It is that part of you that is the repository of all your life experiences and all your hopes and dreams. Alchemized over the years from lead into pure gold, your Inner Samurai is your greatest source of strength and knowing. It is the seat of your wisdom. It is also the place of your extraordinary uniqueness.

The interesting thing about your Inner Samurai is that it speaks to you. Well, maybe not speaks. "Pulses" is a better word. Your Inner Samurai has a gentle, yet very recognizable, way of communicating with you. I like to call it "pulsing." When you go inward and ask your Inner Samurai a question, you will feel a "pulse" answering you. This pulse will have one of two distinct qualities. It will feel like either a *yes* or a *no*.

DISCOVERING YOUR INNER SAMURAI

This book is about discovering your Inner Samurai. It was written for the purpose of helping you as an entrepreneurial woman connect to your inner journey. It was written to empower you with the strength you will need to be successful in building a business. It was written to inspire you with helpful, practical, and relevant tips to make it easier to do so. Since I see no reason to reinvent the wheel, I have provided pointers along the way, directing you away from what to avoid, and accelerators pointing you toward what you can do to enhance your success.

This book serves as a guide to those wanting to build a different kind of business — a business from the inside out. From a place inside you that you as a woman intuitively know and understand. From your Inner Samurai place.

If you are an entrepreneurial woman committed to doing work that is meaningful and important, this book is for you. If you see your work as a mission, service, or calling, the stories in this book will inspire you. If you are someone who is highly ethical, service-oriented, and relationship-focused, you are going to find great value in this book.

If financial comfort is important to you and quality of life even more important, then this book is right up your alley. If your goal is to help other people transform their lives and make a difference in the world, then read on.

Mi viaje es tu viaje.

Part I

Dealing with Change

Chapter 1

AND SO I BEGIN...

The two important things I did learn were that you are as powerful and strong as you allow yourself to be, and that the most difficult part of any endeavor is taking the first step, making the first decision.

— Robyn Davidson

On June 29, 2004, I finally did it. I handed in my resignation as associate professor of music and Director of Choral Activities at James Madison University and began packing up the formidable accumulation of books, music, and files from four educational degrees and 24 years of academic life. Distilled onto one little piece of paper that began with the words "Kindly accept my resignation," and ending with "Sincerely," my former life was over.

My new life as an Accidental Pren-her had begun. "Accidental" because I didn't anticipate it happening, and "pren-her" because I always knew I had it in me to be an entrepreneurial woman. In truth, it was an accident by design, though I could not see that at the time.

YIKES! WHAT THE HELL WAS I THINKING?

I bet you have had that thought once or twice in your life, haven't you? Perhaps you've struggled with a decision, going back and forth over what to do a thousand times. Then, the minute you make up your mind — whoosh! The horse is out of the gate and pounding toward the finish line, with you just trying to stay seated, wondering "What the hell just happened?"

Or, you finally make up your mind that you want to do something — and nothing, absolutely nothing, happens. In fact, nothing does happen for a very long time (or at least it appears nothing is happening). Then, just about the time you've almost forgotten about it — whoosh! There you are again, having the ride of your life barreling down the track, horse kicking up dirt as you charge to the finish line shouting "Whoo-hoo!"

Well, that was how I felt that morning as I opened my briefcase, took out my leather embossed notebook folio and slid my resignation letter across the desk to the Dean. I was on my horse, and we were leaving the gate. My hands were shaking, my palms were damp, and I barely trusted my voice to speak. After thanking him for the opportunity to work with such wonderful students, "best wishes," and a round of handshakes, I walked out into the warm Virginia sunlight feeling dazed, light-headed, and — strangely enough — right as rain.

As I stood there beside my car looking back at what had been my professional home for the past four years, I could hear the beginning grumble of the all-too-familiar voice inside my head criticizing: "Now, look what you've gone and done." It rose steadily in volume and intensity the farther I drove away from campus until it was actually barking orders: "Wait! No! Stop! Go Back!"

I had done the unthinkable. I had resigned with no job lined up to go to and only a vague idea of what I was going to do next.

"Let's take a moment to rethink all this, Susan," the voice inside my head cajoled, taking another tack.

Then, just as quickly as it came, that voice was silenced. In the blessed space of that silence, I could hear my calm, inner voice — the voice I call my Inner Samurai — pulse *yes*, followed by a warm, calming, radiating flood of love. (The Inner Samurai has a gentle, yet very recognizable, way of communicating. I like to call it "pulsing." When you go inward and ask your Inner Samurai a question, you will feel a "pulse" answering you. This pulse will have one of two distinct qualities. It will feel like either a *yes* or a *no*.)

Becoming a pren-her seemed, in retrospect, the most natural thing for me to do. However, the trek from resigning from a prestigious academic post to starting my own successful small business turned out to be fraught with more "start-up woes" than "start-up goes."

HAPPINESS IS AN INSIDE JOB

While at first I felt euphoric because I'd been liberated from corporate academia, I was soon slammed by the twin emotions of panic and fear. Since I had always been a full-time, traditionally employed woman, finding myself out of a job with no idea what I would do next was bloody overwhelming. I couldn't tell from one day to the next whether I was going to wake up feeling exhilarated at being free to do, be, and have whatever I wanted, or shocked by disbelief as the reality of what I had done began to sink in. Most of the time, I felt 98% excited and 2% scared.

Or was it 2% excitement and 98% scared? From one moment to the next it could change. That's what makes the process of becoming a pren-her so incredibly intense.

In truth, the act of following my Inner Samurai was not a new experience. I had been listening to her and following her all my life. When I was younger, I used to call her "my still small voice." Then, when I was in my 30s, "the voice within." In my 40s, it became "my inner knower," and now it is "my Inner Samurai." They all mean the same thing. I have heard others call their deep inner knowing God Self, Soul, God Within, and Spirit. No matter what we call it, we all have that voice of inner knowing.

That voice became my Inner Samurai when I realized how strong, vast and powerful my inner voice was. My Inner Samurai could move mountains, leap over tall buildings with a single bound, and stop charging wildebeests in their tracks. One of my clients calls her Inner Samurai her Inner Super Woman. It's all the same.

And So I Begin . . .

Ch. 1

After my resignation, tapping into my Inner Samurai helped me know just what to do next. I needed to move in the general direction of what I wanted — I needed to feel for that pulse.

What was it that I wanted? I wanted to be happy.

My decision to leave academia was a step in that direction. Certainly, there was much raging, fear and doubting from the voice inside my head (a voice which, as we'll explore later, is very different from the knowing voice of the Inner Samurai). Still, I knew the step I had taken was the right step for me. I knew it because all the other times I'd listened to my Inner Samurai and done something apparently crazy (by all outward reckoning), it had all turned out better than expected. In fact, it had turned out perfectly.

Yes! my Inner Samurai pulsed as the feeling of love bathed me from within.

COURAGE: THE ANTI-DRUG

Perhaps you've heard of Ambrose Hollingworth Redmoon. No? Well, he was the one who penned the popular quote: "Courage is not the absence of fear, but rather the judgment that something else is more important than fear." Does that ring a bell? What I discovered when I researched him was that this quote is only the first line of a much larger quote that he "wrote" as a paraplegic from the confines of a wheelchair.

Born in 1933 in Painesville, Ohio, as James Neil Hollingworth, Ambrose was a beatnik, hippie, and former manager of legendary rock band Quicksilver Messenger Service. At the age of 33, he was in a near-fatal car accident that left him confined to a wheelchair, dependent on the care of others. With his former life gone, he turned to writing. Though he struggled to get his writings published and was little known beyond a relatively small circle of mystic followers, Redmoon kept writing until he passed away in 1996. Five years before his death he wrote an article for the fall issue of *Gnosis: A Journal of the Western Inner Traditions*. In it, he gives the entire quote:

> Courage is not the absence of fear, but rather the judgment that something else is more important than one's fear. The timid presume it is lack of fear that allows the brave to act when the timid do not. But to take action when one is not afraid is easy. To refrain when afraid is also easy. To take action regardless of fear is brave.[1]

We all know of times when, in the midst of abject fear, people perform courageous acts. We've all read the stories of a mother whose son was trapped underneath an overturned tractor. Desperate, and focused only on saving her son's life, she lifted the heavy farm tractor with one hand while rescuing her son with the other. Urban myth? On the contrary, these things happen all the time.

You and I both know what fear feels like. We know how debilitating it is, how it can stop us in our tracks, and how it can make us run away. The courage I am talking about — the courage a mother has when her child needs her — has to do with making the decision that something else is more important than fear. In the case of the mother rescuing her child, it was a matter of her taking action *beyond the reach* of fear by moving in the direction of what she wanted. It wasn't about ignoring her fear. It was about choosing something greater.

In my case, I was choosing happiness. And my first step, after breaking the news to my parents, was to leave the ivory tower — resigning from my academic post took courage. Staying would have been giving in to fear. Giving in to fear would have meant that I had chosen to live a life of complacency, and living that kind of life was no kind of life for me. So, with the voice inside my head raging on and totally freaking out, I moved my hand out *beyond the reach* of fear and grabbed the hand of happiness.

On one level, resigning from academia seemed absolutely nuts. On the other hand, knowing what I know now, it was perfectly natural. However, it was one of the hardest decisions of my life. Still, it was the single most important decision I made in 2004. It meant that I was leaving behind two choirs of wonderful musicians whom I adored and thoroughly enjoyed making music with, as well as a handpicked group of graduate choral conducting students who were bright, fun, and talented. It meant leaving behind the world of academia I had known since I was a child to reach *beyond the reach* of fear for something more.

LINEAGE OF THE IVORY TOWER

I come from a long line of professors. The world of academia and teaching is in my blood. My great-grandfather, Dr. Reid T. Stewart, was a professor of engineering at the University of

Pittsburgh. Among other things, he was interested in steel and was a well-known engineering authority of the time. I was born at the University of Virginia while my father was Chairman of the Departments of Counseling and Guidance. My Momacita (my dad's second wife and my "second mother" who raised me from age six onward), had been an assistant professor of education at the University of Pittsburgh.

Dad and Momacita used to tell a cute story of how they first met. Though they had been aware of each other in faculty meetings for quite some time, they had not been formally introduced. Because of their difference in rank and being from separate departments, opportunity had not presented itself for their meeting. Dad was a full professor and Coordinator of the Rehabilitation Counselor Training Program, and Momacita was a new faculty member and assistant professor in the Education Department. One day, while Momacita was walking in and Dad was walking out through the revolving doors of the Cathedral of Learning, their eyes met. "Hello, Dr. Reid," my soon-to-be new mom said as they entered the turn-style. "Hello, Dr. Bernardo," my dad politely replied upon his exit. Intrigued, Momacita soon arranged for him to be invited to dinner at the home of a mutual friend. The rest, as they say, is history.

Family life revolved around the University of Pittsburgh. I have many fond memories of taking the bus after school to Pitt to draw on the blackboards or do my homework in the "grown-up" desks with seats attached. To amuse myself until my parents came to collect me, I would go to the board with a piece of chalk in my hand, pretending

And So I Begin... Ch. 1

I was a professor teaching a whole classroom of students how to add, subtract, and write in cursive. Sometimes, I was even invited to sit in the back of the room when my parents were lecturing. Enthralled by the professor-student interactions, I was held captive by the debates, the discussions, and the discourse. I loved it!

When I was a little older, I became quite interested in swimming. In addition to taking swim classes at the downtown Pittsburgh YMCA, I also took lessons at Indiana University of Pennsylvania's indoor pool while my dad taught Saturday classes. I took my Basic Water Safety course and Canoe Instructor classes there. Diving to the bottom of the pool to rescue 10-pound bricks and bailing out canoes filled with water was all a part of going to school with Dad. During the summers, when my parents were both visiting professors at the University of Mississippi, I mastered butterfly and flip turns in Ole Miss's outdoor pool in between going to *Planet of the Apes* movies.

All of this left its imprint upon me. Education and learning were an important part of the Reid family lifestyle. They still are. So when I left academia, it seemed quite an unanticipated and surprising move to most people. Some expressed their concern, saying "You know, Susan, maybe you just need some time off. Take a sabbatical." Others were speechless that I would leave a perfectly good job without first securing another post. Then, there were those who thought what I was doing was great and cheered me on, saying "I so wish I had the guts to do what you are doing!" Or, "If I were ten years younger, I would do the same!" The comments that meant the most to me were from those who had done the same thing I was doing and had come out the other side in one piece. They were the first ones to sagely counsel "Susan, life is too short to waste on being unhappy. Follow your heart and be true to you." Thank you!

What's Behind Curtain Number One, Monty?

So here it was — the summer of 2004. I had had a spiritual awakening (more on that later on), had resigned from my academic position, didn't particularly have much of an idea what I was going to do, and didn't know where I was going. Wow, how many of you have felt like that? If you are reading this book, I bet you know exactly what I am talking about!

What did you do to help yourself when you faced a similarly confusing and uncertain time? Did you look to family and friends for help? Many of us do. Did you seek solace in shopping, drinking, or other activities? Perhaps you went into action and immediately shot out your killer résumé or curriculum vitae and started making calls, searching for leads. Or did you do what I did? Did you immediately look for some Divine interaction?

If you are like me, and I suspect you are (if the title of this book is one of the reasons you are reading), then you, too, have probably looked for signs from the Divine. Being the modern girl that I am, I wasn't looking for a burning bush. I figured a Divine fax or memo would do just fine.

And So I Begin... Ch. 1

I cannot tell you how many times during the day I would say aloud, "Anytime now, God. Send me a sign. Show me what to do next!" Partly said in jest, mostly said in earnest, I *was* looking for a sign.

This is about as good a time as any to say that, when I use the word "God" throughout this book, I do mean God, though not in the traditional meaning of the word. I consider God to be within me, not the old man in white robes with a long white beard keeping track of all my rights and wrongs. That was the God of my Presbyterian upbringing.

The God I'm talking about in this book has neither gender, name, nor form. The closest term that expresses its meaning is "Ein Sof," a Kabalistic term meaning "without end," denoting "boundlessness."

As you read this book, you will see me use various words or phrases meaning God. Please feel free to substitute any other word or phrase, such as Source, Universe, Spirit, the Infinite, the Divine, Universal Thought, All That Is — whatever would be meaningful to you. Additionally, my use of the word God is not, in any way, to be misconstrued to mean the exclusion of Allah, Buddha, or anyone or anything that is representational of an All-Knowing Presence.

Getting back to the story — not only did I talk to God when I was alone, I also cracked up my friends with statements such as, "Maybe there's something wrong with my fax line." Or (and this was one of my favorite lines), "By any chance, did God give you a memo today for me?" Though everyone chuckled when I'd say such things, I could tell that they understood what I meant because they, too, were secretly wishing for a fax or memo from God.

Soon, I was desperate. I expanded my request to include messages ranging from carrier pigeons to angelic beings. I wasn't picky. I was even willing to go to some effort to obtain this message, and would gladly have climbed to the top of a mount for some tablets! All I wanted was a sign. "Just send me a sign!"

God, I am sure, was amused.

Then one day, while I was despondently watching an episode of *The West Wing*, I got my memo. The character "Father Cavanaugh," played by Karl Malden, was telling an allegory I had heard many times before. Perhaps you've heard it, too. There, before my eyes, my Divine memo was delivered through a TV program:

> You know, you remind me of the man that lived by the river. He heard a radio report that the river was going to rush up and flood the town and that all the residents should evacuate their homes. But the man said 'I'm religious. I pray. God loves me. God will save me.' The waters rose up. A guy in a row boat came along and he shouted 'Hey, hey you! You in there. The town is flooding. Let me take you to safety.' But the man shouted back 'I'm religious. I pray. God loves me. God will save me.' A helicopter was hovering overhead. And a guy with a megaphone shouted 'Hey you, you down there. The town is flooding. Let me drop this ladder and I'll take you to safety.' But the man shouted back that he was religious, that he prayed, that God loved him and that God will take him to safety. Well . . . the man drowned. And standing at the gates of St. Peter, he demanded an audience with God. 'Lord,' he said, 'I'm a religious man, I pray. I thought you

loved me. Why did this happen?' God said 'I sent you a radio report, a guy in a rowboat, and a helicopter. What the hell are you doing here?'[2]

Everyone on the show laughed. But not me. I was dumbstruck. For months I had been asking for a sign. For months nothing had happened. Then — whoosh! In the space of the time it took for Father Cavanaugh to tell the story, I had gone from 0-200 miles per hour. With my body pressed against the back of the seat, hair flying everywhere, and a grin a mile wide across my face, I knew for sure that I had received my sign. Though not exactly as I had imagined it, it sure was a prime-time message — all pun intended.

While I was vegging-out in front of the TV with less than anything going on in my life, I got my memo. Not only did I get my sign, I was also slammed with full realization. Even though I couldn't see evidence with my physical eyes that God had been listening or that there was anything being done upon my behalf, there had been lots going on behind the scenes. When I had thought nothing was happening, it was just an illusion. There had been many things happening behind the scenes. And with that realization, I felt my Inner Samurai pulse *yes*.

THE UNCERTAIN CERTAINTY OF IT ALL

One morning, not long after my *West Wing* experience, I decided to revisit the day of my spiritual awakening, this time with notebook and pen in hand. I was interested in recording what happened that day and putting my experience into words. I began by using a four-line gata I had heard

Vietnamese monk, Thich Naht Hahn, instruct his students to use when preparing for meditation:

> Breathing in I calm my body and mind.
> Breathing out I smile.
> Dwelling in the present moment;
> I know this is the only moment.

As I settled into my body while focusing on my breath, I felt my body and mind become calm as a serene smile curled the edges of my mouth. I remembered that, on the day of my spiritual awakening, I had been deeply meditating on the oneness of all when — whoosh! My mental state suddenly shifted. One minute I was focused on oneness, and the next, expansiveness. Without preamble or forewarning, my mind spontaneously and instantaneously broke open with a vastness and expansiveness brand new to me. Time stopped. I had no awareness of my body. I was beyond space and time.

Soon, though, something came into view. In my mind's eye, I saw two thick, coliseum-like white pillars reaching up and down as far as I could see. They reminded me of the Doric columns of the Parthenon in Athens, with the capital made of a circle topped by a square.

I remember the first time I visited the Parthenon many years ago. I had been captivated by the strength and beauty of those magnificent columns. That's how I felt as I saw the columns this time, in my mind's eye. Though the columns were quite some distance apart, I could see that there was someone holding each one up. Holding the two pillars in place were two magnificent beings — archangels. They were tall and robust, like Rubens' archangels. Both were bathed in and radiating light. Where they started and the columns ended, I could not tell. They looked right at me, glowing with great love.

While I watched, the archangel columns began positioning themselves on either side of me. Then, coming closer and closer together until the archangels and the columns were inches away from me and the light had increased to such intensity that I thought I would either be squished or obliterated, we merged into one. I was the columns, I was the angelic beings, and I was me, all merged as one. Separation no longer existed. With that realization, my mind exploded outward with a sound and force very much like a sonic boom. Particles of me shot out everywhere, connecting me to everything, everywhere. In truth, I *was* everything, everywhere.

This was my first direct experience with oneness of being, and still, to this day, I have trouble finding the words to adequately describe my experience. Yet, what remained was simpler to explain — the idea that separation is an illusion. Oneness is. All is well and unfolding exactly as it is meant to be. This depth of knowing was so profound my body spilled over in joy. My heart felt so big I thought it would burst right out of my chest. Tears flowed freely down my face as laughter bubbled to the surface. I was bathed in a depth of love and light that was at once familiar and new. Suspended in a state of awareness, I sat in meditation that day for four hours, though it seemed no more than 15 minutes.

For about a week, I remained in this state of blissful awareness. Though I was in body, I knew

I was more than body. The veil between here and there was non-existent. I was living in both places at once. I was both here and there. The veil separating the two was gone. Here and there were one and I freely inhabited both at the same time.

As a result, I felt bigger. In all, I felt 18 feet tall and 12 feet wide. When I looked down, it seemed like my feet were floating about 12 inches above the ground, though when I walked I could feel my feet roll like they always did from heel to toe with each step. When I walked through doorways I instinctively ducked, thinking I was taller than I was. Then, I'd immediately laugh at myself for doing so. My favorite room of my home at this time was my office — the only room in the house with vaulted cathedral ceilings. One of the more amusing moments during this time was thinking as I was getting ready for bed that I'd never be able to fit into my nightshirt because I felt so big!

During this week, I noticed things around me had become richer, fuller, and greatly enhanced. Colors were more vivid. Smells were more piquant. My hearing, always very acute, became even more so. Touch fascinated me. I was enthralled with the energy exchange that occurred when I reached out to touch someone or something. Whenever I got within 12 to 18 inches of what I wanted to touch, two things happened. The first thing was that I could see my energy extending outward like tendrils from my hand toward that which I was intending to touch. The second thing was that what I intended to touch reached back, extending the same kind of wispy energy in the direction of my hand.

I was so fascinated by this exchange of energy that I played with it, totally absorbed, for hours at a time. I could do this with anything, though I found nature and animals the most actively responsive. The energy that danced in the space between my actual physical hand and the thing I intended to touch was alive with color, intensity, and pulsating life. Witnessing this, I remember thinking, "This must be how Jesus healed the sick and caused the lame to walk. He commingled with the energy, affecting the intended result in the space between the actual touch." It was all about the energy!

Well, it didn't take me long to focus my energetic touch in the direction of my sweet cat, Passion. Passion loved to be touched and was a very willing subject for my energetic explorations. As I reached toward her, she reached back. So, too, when she wanted to be touched or otherwise get my attention, she would first reach out to me energetically before she meowed or rubbed against my leg. First the energy, then the touch. First the energetic reaching out, then a physical reaching out would follow. It was all so natural.

The next thing I noticed was that once an energetic encounter was made, energies commingled to test the waters, so to speak. An energetic decision was being made. Sometimes the energies would increase in intensity, strengthening in preparation for physical touch. Other times one or both energies would touch and then recede back to each side. Often, Passion would respond with great enthusiasm when I reached out to pet her, her energetic tendrils leaping enthusiastically toward mine. By contrast, the energy of a bird she was stalking would recede quickly, soon after the first wisp of energy exchange.

ENERGETICALLY PEACEFUL

I was curious to see if I could observe this interaction between people. Therefore, I went people-watching at a park near my home. Sitting comfortably on a park bench, I looked around. Across from me, I spied a lovely young woman enjoying the day, reading a book. She had placed a slightly crumpled brown paper bag on the bench to her left and was absently picking up and biting into an apple, presumably leftover from lunch. After biting, she'd put the apple back down again, chewing contentedly until something she was reading caught her attention. Then she'd pause, mid-chew, to concentrate. Energetically, she looked peaceful. Physically, she looked relaxed and fully engaged in her reading, rarely looking up to glance about.

Then along came a nice-looking young man. (You knew this part was coming, didn't you?) He spotted and took an immediate interest in the young woman. With one quick glance to the right and another to the left, he sat down on the left side of her bench. The woman didn't look up. The man, by contrast, was openly checking her out. I could see the energy around him amping up, getting ready to expand, but their energy had not yet made contact, so she gave him no notice.

Next, he opened his backpack, pulled out a sketchbook and a pencil, and began sharpening the tip with a great display of activity. He stole a few surreptitious looks at his bench mate to see whether

And So I Begin . . . — Ch. 1

she had taken any notice of him and soon settled into position. With his body turned in her direction, focusing his gaze slightly ahead of and to the left of her, he began to sketch.

I was fascinated. Neither paid me any attention. But, watching their energetic and physical interaction was mesmerizing. She, fully absorbed in her book, and he, fully absorbed in her — though pretending to be otherwise. I chuckled to myself, feeling very much like a clandestine interloper. Try as he might to get her attention, his bench partner was not paying him any mind. That is, until his amped up energy expanded several feet out from him in her direction, and the initial energetic encounter was made. Tendrils tentatively meeting, they had their first energy exchange as I watched. The way the tips of their energy tendrils met was gentle and exploratory. Energetic information was exchanged very quickly and I could see a rippling disturbance in her energetic field. In accord, the young woman shifted in her seat, still taking no direct notice of the young man.

Not to be deterred, the young man turned his body more in her direction, picked up his sketchbook, and began drawing her silhouette. While doing so, his energy expanded outward even further in her direction, and the quality of it was more intense. Now he had her attention. She shifted more visibly this time, uncrossed and recrossed her legs, and smiled distractedly in his direction while pulling her lunch bag closer to her. Her energy had completely receded and her body followed suit.

Encouraged by her glance in his direction and completely ignoring the quality of her smile, he verbally pressed on. "Hi, my name is Mark. Isn't it a beautiful day?"

"Yes, it is." She darted a bothered look in his direction then ducked her head quickly back into her book. I could see that her energetic field was quite compact, dense, almost protective, and much closer to her body now. In agreement, her body turned away from the young man as she transferred the book from her left to her right hand. Her left arm crossed protectively across her stomach, resting tensely in the crook of her right arm.

Mark's energy had receded upon first contact with the young woman. Unaware of this, and oblivious to her body language, he put down his sketchbook, all pretense of drawing aside. He asked "So, what are you reading?"

Silence. Thirty seconds passed. I heard the distant sound of ducks on the pond.

Then — energetic mistake of mistakes, he slid several inches toward her, still hoping to engage her. My mouth dropped in disbelief. "Hey buddy," I wanted to counsel, "don't you see a train wreck in the making? You are about to have your hopes dashed. Back away from the girl!"

Instead, I heard him say, "Hey, be nice now. Tell me what you are reading." And with that, her energetic field decidedly compressed around her. She stood up and walked away briskly. Left behind were a brown paper bag, a half-eaten apple, and a baffled and miffed young man.

"Amazing," I said aloud, releasing the breath I had been holding.

Pay Attention

This was a moment of meaningful revelation for me. The occurrence in the park showed me the importance of paying attention to my energy and paying attention to what is going on inside of me. The couple on the park bench showed me that, long before any outer exchange, manifestation, or experience takes place, an inner energetic exploration for resonance and alignment has to occur.

That's when I knew that what may seem like chance meetings, strange coincidences, or unexpected events are not random accidents. They are accidents by design!

I picked up my belongings and left the park. I began thinking about how, by focusing on and making choices that lined up with my happiness, I had unleashed the powers of the Universe. Now those powers were orchestrating great movement and a brand new manifestation — a brand new now.

Notes from Your Inner Samurai

It all begins when the soul would have its way with you.

— Ralph Waldo Emerson

- Most new beginnings come at the end of a crash and burn experience.

- Rethink endings. It isn't that something has ended. It's that something new has begun.

- Accidents are never random. They are accidents by design.

- You determine your happiness — not someone or something outside of you.

- Remember the words of Ambrose Hollingworth Redmoon: "Courage is not the absence of fear, but rather the judgment that something else is more important than one's fear."

- When God sends you a rowboat, climb in.

- Know that there are great and powerful forces acting on your behalf, even if you have not yet seen physical manifestation.

- Trust that everything is unfolding exactly as it is meant to be.

Chapter 2

Now What?

*We must be willing to get rid of the life we've
planned, so as to have the life that is waiting for us.*

— Joseph Campbell

That's Great! So What Are You Up to Now?

By August of 2004, I was in uncharted waters. Here it was, the start of a new academic year, and for the first time since kindergarten I was not, in one way or another, involved with school. I was neither going to school, getting ready to teach at school, nor involved with students preparing to go back to school. It felt weird not to be doing the familiar things I was so used to doing at this time of year. It also felt very freeing.

For the first time in my life, I wasn't feeling stressed, pressured, or anxious about the start of a school year. I wasn't feeling that rush of excitement about going back to school, meeting new students, and greeting old ones, either. For the first time in many years, I hadn't spent my summer choosing music, writing syllabi, and wondering how many tenors I would have in my choir. Instead, I had spent my time off in a more relaxed and peaceful mode, writing, reading, hanging out with friends, and spending time with my parents. It was a remarkable moment in time for me. It was magical and precious.

Who Am I Now?
Good Question

While sitting at my kitchen table one morning, drinking raspberry tea, I heard the local school bus pull up outside, stopping just long enough for the neighborhood children to pile aboard. With fingers of both hands curled idly around the comforting warmth of my mug and with the aroma of sweet raspberries tickling my nose, I paused and listened for the bus to continue on its way. There, in the space between the school bus loading and the next sip of tea, I wondered to myself "Who am I?" or more specifically, "Who am I now?"

Have you ever had that experience? When the most profound question arises, seemingly out of nowhere, causing a major life review and leaving you in a suspended state. Contemporary spiritual teacher Eckhart Tolle humorously calls that state "the dash between the birth and death dates of our lives." Yogis reverently refer to this as the pause between the inhalation and exhalation of breath. I call it the place where all possibilities exist.

As the school bus pulled away with its familiar release of air brakes and roaring engine, I waited in anticipation of the answer to my question. I waited, and waited some more. Nothing. (You knew that was coming.) So, I asked again, this time aloud, "Who am I?" Silence. More waiting. I took another tack. Instead of "who am I", I asked, "Who *was* I?"

Relief washed over me. Now that was a question the voice inside my head could answer. I was no longer the Director of Choral Activities. Check. I was no longer an employee of the great Commonwealth of Virginia. Check, check. Okay, this is going well, I thought as I took another sip of tea, its heat warming my throat. I no longer work for a university. Check. I no longer have a boss. Yeah! I smiled at that one as I reached for a piece of freshly buttered toast. Keep going. No one was calling the shots for me and no one was expecting anything of me.

Hmm. What did *that* mean? I paused in mid-chew.

LOTUS FLOWER OPENING

"No one is calling the shots for me and no one is expecting anything of me," I said aloud, testing the air to see how that sounded. Then I felt it. Huh?!? What was that? There it was again, that odd sensation beneath my sternum like petals of some great flower opening, slowly, one at a time. What a peculiar feeling. When was the last time I had felt something like this, I mused?

No one is calling the shots for me and no one is expecting anything of me, I thought again, pausing to see what would happen. Then, as if on cue, another petal gently unfolded. What's so special about that phrase? I repeated it again. How come each time I think it another petal opens? Then it dawned on me: there had always been someone else, a person in authority, calling the shots for me and about my life, all my life. From the simple things like telling me that I had to finish my peas before I could have dessert, to the more complex issues like what college would be best for me, there had always been someone else who had either decided these things for me, or heavily influenced me. Then, as I grew older, without giving it much thought, I transferred that responsibility to my bosses.

Sure, I had been the independent sort. I had made many decisions autonomous of others. However, when it came down to the big decisions, I had always made them by either relying on the advice of others, or by keeping what I knew they would advise in mind. And here's the real kicker. Until that moment, I had not even known I had done so, or, at least, not to the full extent. In fact, if you had asked me earlier, I would have said without a moment's hesitation, "Of course, I'm an independent thinker. I definitely make my own decisions."

I suddenly realized the absurdity of that assumption. But now, now things were different. I was different. From this moment forward, I realized I was the one fully responsible for calling the shots, if I even cared to call any shots at all. I was ushering in a brand new era. With each petal opening I could feel myself morphing from someone who had worked all her life, living up to the expectations of others and the voice inside her head, into someone who was willing to chart her own course, guided by her own stars. The great flower slowly opening was . . . me.

Wow! For the first time in my life, I was *really* calling the shots. What an amazing feeling. Before,

Now What?

Ch. 2

I had listened to many voices inside and outside of my head. Now, I was listening to one. Now, I was listening to the great voice within, my Inner Samurai. As I sipped my tea, contemplatively nibbling around the edges of my buttered toast, a new thought arose: Susan, you can be anyone you want to be. Another petal uncurled. Who do you want to be, now?

Good question to have at the start of a new school year. "Good question," I said to the now vacant spot where my neighborhood school children had once stood. As a reminder to myself, I called after them, "Remember to be who you are."

ARE YOU MY MOTHER?

By August, I had already started down the sole proprietor path by starting up and launching *Full Score Conducting* — my freelance conducting business. It seemed the logical thing to do. After all, I had been successfully conducting choirs and orchestras all my adult life. Conducting was something I knew very well. I loved doing it, teaching it, and watching it. After nearly 25 years in the music world, I knew lots of people and had great networking connections already in place. Plus, I had plenty of gigs lined up to get me started on my path as a freelance conductor. It just seemed like the natural next step for me.

Within just a few months, I had morphed from making wonderful music with choirs, employed by a university, to making wonderful music with choirs, employed by myself. I loved my new boss — me! She was organized, creative, and fun. She knew what she wanted, kept the lines of communication open, and was on top of things. I loved working for her. Best of all, I loved what I was doing. I was conducting choirs and orchestras and working with music educators, adjudicating, and coaching. I was free as a bird, traveling here and there, doing exactly what I wanted to do. My friends who worked at traditional 9-to-5 jobs envied me. They also wondered what I did all day.

Somewhere along the way I realized that all the activity I was engaged in wasn't who *I was*. It was simply what I was *doing*. So, just who was I now? That question haunted me by day and stalked me by night. I pondered that question over and over, like a honeybee in search of nectar, all day, every day. You see, the problem was that I had grown so accustomed to identifying myself by what I had, what I did, and what I had accomplished — I had lost sight of *me*.

Not only had I lost sight of who I was in the past, I wasn't all that sure who I was in the present. It wasn't how much I earned or what others thought of me. That's what I used to think. Since who I was had been built around and upon the labels, titles, and achievements I had earned, it was difficult for me to see myself in any other way. Who was I *now*? And what did I want most?

I couldn't remember the last time I had thought about those questions, and I was beginning to wonder if I ever had. Now, they kept ringing in my ears and bouncing around inside my head. Until my current spiritual awakening, I had quite forgotten that I was, as author and speaker Wayne Dyer so eloquently puts it: "a unique portion of the essence of God."[1] I had forgotten about that part of me. Not only that, I had confused that part of me for outer labels and trappings. In short, I had substituted myself for things and thoughts.

Therefore, by September, 2004, I found myself in the midst of a full-blown identity crisis. Who am I? What do I want most? These questions addled my mind so much that soon I felt like the little bird in P. D. Eastman's beloved children's book, *Are You My Mother?* Do you know that story? It's a wonderful story of a greatly confused baby bird who hatches from his egg while his mother is out scratching around for food. Because he hatches alone, with no siblings in site, the poor little guy can't figure out who he is. He doesn't know his identity.

Throughout the story, he (could be she; we aren't really sure) walks around meeting various insects, animals, and even a tractor while searching for his mother. No matter who he meets or who he asks, the answer is always the same: "No, dear, I am not your mother." Soon, the baby bird starts feeling anxious and begins to panic. "Are you my mother? Are you my mother?" he urgently asks. "No, I am not your mother." Finally, the baby bird does find his mother. For a time, though, the reader is uncertain whether or not the story will end happily.

I could relate to the baby bird. I didn't know who I was. It was as if I had just hatched. All the titles I had collected and things I had earned were just pointing me back to the self I assumed myself to be. Now it was time for me to find me. It was time for me to walk around my little world and look for clues as to what my unique portion of God's essence was all about.

LISTENING TO WHAT MATTERS

Okay. Let's review, I said to myself one day. I am a unique portion of God's essence. Right. Now what? My personal identity crisis continued. Months raged on. I reviewed my life from every angle looking for answers. I scoured family picture albums in search of clues. I looked to my parents and friends for crumbs of insight into who I was. I read books, took personality tests, and even consulted the stars. I was desperate. I looked everywhere I knew — outside myself — for the answers.

Finally, I remembered. Not so long ago, I vowed to make my Inner Samurai the dominant voice I listened to. How easily I had forgotten! How easily I had turned to my outer world for answers. I had forgotten to go within. Now, I knew what to do. It was time for me to quit seeking answers outside myself and go inward. Inward to hear the answers that I knew would come from my Inner Samurai. Inward to consult the one with all the answers: me, myself, and I. I? Yes. My Inner Samurai, of course!

I know you can relate to my experience. You know what it's like to look outside yourself for answers, don't you? It's all about thinking someone or something else knows the answer better than you do. Up until the summer of 2004, I did that on a regular basis. I looked outside of myself for the answers that were there all the time — inside of me.

How about you? How long have you been looking outside yourself for the answers to your inner questions? We all do it sometimes. Partly, because we don't quite trust in ourselves to come up with the answers. And partly we do it because we think other people know best. Combined, these ingredients make for a looking-outside-yourself cocktail that is lethal — yes, it might kill you. Regardless of whether it actually sounds the death knell, though, at the very least it will render you powerless. Powerless to make decisions. Powerless to find your own answers. Powerless to stand unwavering in your truth. When we look outward for the answers, we take ourselves farther and farther away from the place of our greatest knowing.

This book is about discovering your Inner Samurai. That part of you that is the repository of all your life experiences and all your hopes and dreams. Alchemized over the years from lead into pure gold, your Inner Samurai is your greatest source of strength and knowing. It is the seat of your wisdom. It is also the place of your extraordinary uniqueness.

THE WORLD IS MY OYSTER

What did I find when I went inward, seeking my Inner Samurai? Probably the same thing you will find, too. That we are all free to be anything and anyone we want to be. We can be trash collectors, book store owners, or chemical engineers. We can live as recluses, celebrities, or royalty. We can save the whales, fight for our country, or meditate on the tops of mountains. When we know we are free to be, then we know that "the world is my oyster," as English poet and playwright William Shakespeare penned in *The Merry Wives of Windsor*.

That's the beauty of going inward. That's the advantage of discovering the truth of who you are. Each of us is a unique portion of the essence of God, and each of us is free to be. Free to do amazing good in this world and free to wreak havoc. Free to travel the world over and free to stay close to home. Free to be wildly successful and free to just get by. "Free to be" means that the world truly is your oyster. And that, my friends, is one heck of a freeing feeling.

Freed from the outer expectations of others and the voice inside my head, I was now able to decide who I wanted to be. Instead of looking outward for the answers, I looked within. Now I could choose how I wanted to show up in the world. Instead of turning to others to figure out who I was, I turned inward to decide that for myself. Here is the revelation that came to me: It isn't a matter of figuring out who you are or what you need to do; it's about being who you are and letting the rest take care of itself.

This bears repeating: *It's about being who you are and letting the rest take care of itself.*

Being who I am as a unique portion of the essence of God means that what I do won't be limited to a specific job or career slot. Being who I am means that manifestations of what I do will be varied, change over time, and evolve as I grow. Being who I am means that there is no goal that needs to be reached, nothing to attain, and no one outside myself that I need to please. Being who I am means being free.

I can be a unique portion of God's essence and let the rest take care of itself. No worries about how something will occur. No need to fret about or manipulate things to make them happen. As Mike Dooley, creator of Truly Unique Thoughts® says, "Let the Universe take care of the dreaded hows." Our job is to be who we are — unique portions of God's essence.

FREE TO BE

The final four months of 2004 were momentous for me. Much to my surprise, I had gone through and survived a full-blown identity crisis. Surprised that I had even needed to do so, my mind now played catch up to my newly integrated self. Going through that identity crisis and coming out the other side in touch with who I am and what I most desire was a powerfully liberating and freeing experience.

From this new vantage point, I could now look back upon my life and see that every bend in the path and every fork in the road had been there for a reason. All those hairpin turns were there so I could more easily climb the hills and mountains of my life. Each long expansive stretch of roadway was there so I could reach my destination quickly and effortlessly. I could now see the perfection of the path I had taken. Every boulder, ice storm, sunny day, and cloud in the sky had been exactly what I needed it to be, to get me from Point A to B, from where I was to where I am now.

For the first time in my life, I had no desire to go back and do anything over. I saw my life for the perfection that it was and didn't want to change a thing. I no longer regretted choices I'd made, conversations I'd had, or things I'd done. I was free. I was free to live a life of no regrets. I was free from my past and free from my future. My past ceased to be a book with no ending and became, instead, a rich treasure trove of memories and experiences that I could revisit any time, though I no longer felt the need to dwell upon them. What was done was done. Anything left undone, I now knew, would take care of itself in the fullness of time.

I was free! Better said, I had been free all along and was just realizing it. "Duh," I exclaimed as the heel of my hand lightly smacked my forehead. "It was there all along! The beautiful gift I thought I had just now opened was there waiting for me all along!" I laughed aloud. I shook my head in disbelief. I was free — had always been. New and not new. Ah, the sweet dichotomy of that thought.

So, what could — what would — I do with this new beginning? What would you do? Knowing that you could be anyone you wanted to be and do anything you wanted to do, what would you choose? It's a daunting prospect, this freedom. In the end, the decision was easy for me. I would be happy. I would live a richly authentic life based on and in alignment with the greater knowing of who I knew myself to be.

Notes from Your Inner Samurai

> *When I was going through my transition of being famous, I tried to ask God why was I here? What was my purpose? Surely, it wasn't just to win three gold medals. There has to be more to this life than that.*
>
> — Wilma Rudolph

- Big change often feels like death; as if an old part of us must die in order for the new part to be born. The birthing of something new does require a deep integration. Some things will cease to be. Others will take on new form. Allow the process.

- It is never too late to start down another path, pursue your dream, or do what you want to do. Ever.

- You are what you think you are. You bring into manifestation the things you think about. While you're doing all this thinking, don't forget who you are — a unique portion of God's essence.

- Make your Inner Samurai the primary voice you listen to. Turn to others for support. Turn inward for guidance.

- Today, begin living your life of no regrets. No need to wait until tomorrow.

- Be who you are and let the rest take care of itself.

Chapter 3

THE SHIFT

It's exhilarating to be alive in a time of awakening consciousness; it can also be confusing, disorienting, and painful.

— Adrienne Rich

NEW WAYS OF THINKING AND BEING

All spiritual awakenings come with major shifts in perception and perspectives. That's putting it mildly! In actuality, having a spiritual awakening is like riding the Kraken roller coaster at Sea World in Orlando, Florida. I know. I did it. Twice! Named after the legendary sea monster of gargantuan size, the Kraken took me for a ride — lifting me higher, dropping me lower, and spiraling me faster than any other roller coaster I had ever been on.

Seated in a floorless car, I kept telling myself the ride's over-the-shoulder restraint would hold me in. What came next was a 15-story death-defying plunge that mercilessly wrangled an involuntary thrill scream out of me. Hurtling along at 65 miles an hour over more than 4,000 miles of steel track — with seven inversions thrown in just for kicks — I held on to my restraint for dear life! First, there was the vertical loop, then the dive loop, followed by the zero-G and cobra rolls, ending with the corkscrew to finish me off. In a little over two minutes, my 90 minutes of disgruntled time standing in line under the blazing Florida sun was transformed into a rapturous smile. "Let's go again!" was all I could say.

Yep. That pretty much describes a spiritual awakening. It's a roller coaster — don't let anyone tell you differently. When a spiritual awakening occurs, it will bring about major shifts in your life. No aspect of your life is spared. Relationships, money, career, personal belief systems, and living conditions all get a major overhaul. Your whole world is turned upside down and inside out. A spiritual awakening is the biggest ride of your life. It is normal to feel rolled, looped and spiraled. It's an unsettling time. It's also a joyous time.

From Outer Thinking To Inner Awareness

I found three things to be immensely helpful as I went through the turbulence of my spiritual awakening. The first thing was to repeat this phrase: *Everything that is arising, shifting, and changing is for my highest good and greatest well-being*, as often as possible. Whenever I became aware of the voice inside my head trying to figure out what was happening or where I was going, I did the second thing: I gently brought myself back to the present moment by saying aloud: "All is well." The third thing I did was breathe. Just breathe.

Deep centering breaths were especially helpful when I'd hear the voice inside my head telling me that I should lift off from my current experience and come back to it later, when I was better able to handle it. By contrast, whenever I would check in with my Inner Samurai, all I felt was inner love and bubbling joy. I never had any feeling of alarm from my Inner Samurai. Instead, I'd feel the *yes* pulse, even amidst the trauma that was unfolding in my personal life.

Why is there all this turbulence around a spiritual awakening? In one word: ego. During a spiritual awakening, inner awareness is becoming the primary way of being, while outer thinking is becoming secondary. This is a complete reversal of the way things have been for the ego. Since it is used to ruling the roost, so to speak, the ego will experience your spiritual awakening as death.

Awakening your spirit is not really death to the ego, though. Instead, it's putting your ego in its rightful place — secondary to your spiritual, inner awareness. Second to your Inner Samurai. As contemporary spiritual teacher Eckhart Tolle eloquently explains:

> When that shift happens, which is the shift from thinking to awareness, intelligence far greater than the ego's cleverness begins to operate in your life. Emotions and even thoughts become depersonalized through awareness. Their impersonal nature is recognized. There is no longer a self in them. They are just human emotions, human thoughts. Your entire personal history, which is ultimately no more than a story, a bundle of thoughts and emotions, becomes of secondary importance

and no longer occupies the forefront of your consciousness. It no longer forms the basis for your sense of identity. You are the light of Presence, the awareness that is prior to and deeper than any thoughts and emotions.[1]

This is why it is so important to do what you can to quiet your mind and let your spiritual awakening unfold, as naturally as possible. To do that, all you need to do is recognize what's going on when the voice inside your head — your ego — starts kicking up. Then move into observation mode.

Observation mode is a place where you have a bird's eye view of what's going on. It's a place where you can observe what's happening. One of my clients puts herself in observation mode by saying, "Hmm . . . well, that's certainly interesting," when her ego starts clamoring for attention. Another acknowledges what's being said with a quick, "Thanks for sharing," followed closely by, "I've got it now, thanks." Still another breaks the flow of chatter by laughing out loud, then saying, "You'll be okay. I've got your back."

What I like about how all three of my clients deal with the voice inside their heads is that they recognize that their thoughts are just passing phenomena. They don't attach to their thoughts, though they do acknowledge them. They stay in observation mode and don't take their thoughts too seriously. I see their use of humor as healthy.

NON-EGO-BASED POINT OF VIEW

What happens if you don't quiet your mind? Same thing that happens if you don't relax into the experience of the roller coaster — instead of the fun ride it's supposed to be, it becomes terrifying. At best, you will end up trying to control your spiritual awakening and bring it to an end before it's time. At worst, you will think you have gone crazy.

Abraham Maslow, father of humanistic psychology and the originator of the now famous *Hierarchy of Needs*, once stated: "What is necessary to change a person is to change his awareness of himself." In order to do this we must develop a non-ego-based point of view.

This point of view is one in which we recognize and understand that the ego has virtually no power or control over us or what happens to us. There are so many body functions that our ego has nothing to do with. For instance, our body grows, develops, changes, and declines all by itself, without any input from ego. We breathe, swallow, cough and sneeze without any involvement from ego. We are birthed into this world and birthed out of this world because of something more than ego, not as a consequence of ego. The voice inside our head, though, would have us think differently.

THE DOORWAY TO AWARENESS

Just think about it: The ego is powerless over you. *Powerless!* That is, until you start forming attachments to your thoughts and giving them meaning. That's when the ego kicks in, becoming identified with the meaning. That's how the ego forms an attachment. The ego doesn't know itself and is never in the present moment. Its domains are the past and the future. It thinks compulsively, in order to be assured of its future existence. The extent of the ego's inability to recognize itself and see what it is doing, is staggering.

Awareness, by contrast, lives only in the present — never in the past or future. It derives genuine power from being present. All you need to do to tap into this awareness is observe your thoughts and emotions as they come up. Simply observe them as the natural rising and passing away of the phenomena that they are. No need to do anything about them. No need to attach and hold on to them as if you were freeze-framing one frame in a movie. Simply allow them to pass, like clouds in the sky. This kind of alert observation or seeing is what Vietnamese monk Thich Naht Hahn calls *mindfulness*. Contemporary spiritual teacher Baba Ram Dass calls it *being here now*.

What does this mean for you? It could mean nothing. It could mean everything! It's entirely up to you. Perhaps you will begin experimenting with awareness by observing the myriad thoughts and feelings bombarding you each day as if they were merely clouds passing in the sky. "Hmm, that's interesting. How about that?" Do this without any attachment to the outcome, and you will be amazed at what hooks you and begs for attachment. If you can do this, for even a couple seconds at a time, you will have opened the doorway to awareness. That, my friends, is the doorway inward — inward to your Inner Samurai.

ATTACHMENT TO THOUGHTS

Remember, though, there is no place for the voice inside your head when you are being present in the now. Therefore, your ego will do everything in its power to re-attach you to thoughts and feelings from the past and fears about the future in a desperate attempt to get you to focus anywhere else but in the present.

For the most part, the ego is very successful in getting us to do just that. I bet you know exactly what I am talking about. How many times during the day do you catch yourself thinking about the past or planning for the future? From keeping track of what time you need to leave the house in the morning to beat rush-hour traffic to ruminations on a great lost love, it is so easy for us to shape-shift from the past to the present to the future and back again. We do this incessantly, numerous times a day, mostly on autopilot. Our attention only becomes riveted when our thoughts freeze-frame and focus in on one conversation, event, or fantasy.

For the most part, we spend our time with the babble of our thoughts running in the background of our everyday activities. Half the time, we aren't even aware of what we are thinking about.

Not only that, most of us have been taught to believe that what we are thinking (our unique perspective) is the truth. Not just the truth for us, but the truth for all. We think that the way something happened in the past or the way something is supposed to happen in the future, is true.

Why do we think our thoughts are the truth? Because we form attachments to our thoughts. Instead of listening to our Inner Samurai, we form attachments to what the voice inside our head is telling us. When that happens, we're lost — lost to focusing on past failures or future dividends instead of present joys. Lost to what really matters in life. We dwell within the domain of the ego believing it to be real. When we do, we lose our ability to dance with the winds of heaven.

Dance Like There's Nobody Watching

The good news is that you, in the present, are smarter than your ego chewing over the details of your past or scheming for your future. You, in the present, realize that truth is relative. You, in the present, know that truth is a process, not an event. Above all else, you, in the present, are able to discern that truth is nothing more than a thought, an opinion, and a perspective. This is the knowledge that your Inner Samurai knows. Your Inner Samurai lives in the present, dwells in awareness, and takes great delight in the now. It dances with joy. It is fully aware. Its point of power is only in the now.

If you just sit back and ponder this for a moment, you will see how powerful this kind of knowing really is. Go ahead. Take a moment. Fully take this all in. When you do, something meaningful is going to take place. Something that will change how you view the voice inside your head, forever. You will experience a quantum shift in thinking about how you view the ego, and its role in your life. You will know, with unwavering certainty, that your point of awareness — your only point of genuine power — is in the now.

You will understand that the only hold your past has over you is the power you give it, through your attachments. Your future is being created now, by what you are thinking in the present. Forget about the future. Focus on the now. Let the future take care of itself. As Ram Dass says: "Be here now!"

Spend little time in the future. Spend less time in the past. Be here now, or in the well-known advice of educator and psychologist William W. Purkey:

> Dance like there's nobody watching;
> Love like you'll never get hurt;
> Sing like there's nobody listening;
> Live like it's heaven on earth;
> And speak from the heart to be heard.

NOTES FROM YOUR INNER SAMURAI

Change your thoughts, and in the twinkling of an eye, all your conditions change. Your world is a world of crystallized ideas, crystallized words. Sooner or later, you reap the fruits of your words and thoughts.

— Florence Scovel Shinn

- All spiritual awakenings feel like roller coaster rides. The sooner you accept this, the sooner you will enjoy the ride.

- On your spiritual roller coaster ride, your Inner Samurai is your over-the-shoulder restraint, holding you securely, lovingly, and safely in place so you can get on with enjoying the ride of your life.

- Trust the process and enjoy the journey. Making the shift from thinking to awareness, you're bound to experience a few bumps along the way.

- Do all you can to remain unattached to outcomes. This is the surest way to keep you in your greatest power spot — the present.

- Fretting about the future or worrying about the past is just that: frets and worries. Who needs them?

The Shift

Ch. 3

- Cultivate a non-ego-based point of view and speak from the heart to be heard.

- Dance like there's nobody watching — that's the best feeling of all.

Chapter 4

TAO

You cannot travel the path until you have become the path itself.

— Buddha

YOU CAN'T TELL A BOOK BY ITS COVER

For centuries, Japanese businessmen have used Miyamoto Musashi's *The Book of Five Rings* as a guide for business. If you're familiar with this book, you may be wondering why I'm mentioning it in the same context as women's business success. After all, it has traditionally been associated with the masculine model of doing business.

However, there is much more about *The Book of Five Rings* than meets the eye. It is not just a book for those who want to learn about strategy. It is also a book on Zen philosophy and a manual on how to succeed in life. Most significantly, it is a book about Kwannon, or Guan Yin, the female bodhisattva of compassion. (A bodhisattva in Buddhism is a being who is dedicated to attaining Enlightenment for the sake of others.)

In the introduction to his book, Musashi explains:

> To write this book I did not use the law of Buddha or the teachings of Confucius, neither old war chronicles nor books on martial tactics. I take up my brush to explain the true spirit of this Ichi school as it is mirrored in the Way of heaven and Kwannon.

The Book of Five Rings is an important book for both men and women. It is a challenging book to read, to be sure — dry and formal, lacking in adequate cultural, literary, and philosophical commentary. Because it is a translation, much of the nuance is lost. It is a book that was never intended for just one reading. It was meant to be studied, applied, and studied again and again. For those who are willing to go deeper, there are many gemstones to discover in its pages.

Musashi's Gemstones

Learning to go inward for the answers takes some practice. It also takes some cultivation. Arguably, one of the most famous books on the practice of going inward is *The Book of Five Rings*. It was written over 360 years ago, at a time when feudal Japan was going through a period of great upheaval and social change. The country was united under the Tokugawa Shogunate, although Japan was still struggling to recover from more than four centuries of internal strife. The great provincial armies were disbanded and many samurai were out of work. As a result, numerous samurai were without masters. With nothing else to do, these master-less samurai, called ronin, roamed across Japan looking for other samurai, against whom to test their swords.

Musashi's father was a samurai. Musashi was a ronin living in a society where there was no longer any place for men at arms. Privately, he kept the old ways and the code of the samurai alive by devoting himself to the military arts, specifically to Kendo — "the Way of the sword." Musashi was also much more than a ronin. He was a philosopher, a sculptor, and a sumi-e painter (Sumi-e is a form of Japanese brush painting where only black ink is used, emphasizing white space and lines). He was also a life-long Zen practitioner.

When Musashi was in his 60s, he decided to write down the philosophy that had determined the course of his life path. In *The Book of Five Rings*, he explains nine rules for studying his path. They are:

1. Do not think dishonestly.
2. The Way (path) is in training.
3. Become acquainted with every art.
4. Know the Ways of all professions.
5. Distinguish between gain and loss in worldly matters.
6. Develop intuitive judgment and understanding for everything.
7. Perceive those things that cannot be seen.
8. Pay attention even to trifles.
9. Do nothing that is of no use.

These nine rules are the quintessential distillation of everything that Musashi wanted to tell his readers about how to live their lives. They apply to the outer world of business and to the inner world of your Inner Samurai. In fact, Musashi's steps will help you get in touch with and strengthen your Inner Samurai.

THINK HONESTLY

The first rule, "Do not think dishonestly," is the keystone. When turned around it becomes: "Think honestly." For women this can be a particularly challenging concept to embrace, because it requires you to think honestly, perhaps for the first time in your life, about who you are and what you most want.

Many women are unused to doing this. We are so used to thinking about who we are in relation to other people. We are our mother's daughter, our children's mother, our mate's wife, our sister's sister, and our boss's employee, to name a few. To think honestly about who you are out of context to other people seems foreign to many women. Yet, that is what Musashi is calling you to do.

Think about it. Who are you and what do you most want? How do you desire to live your life? What inspires you? What feeds you? What brings you to life?

What do you want? Go on now. Think big. Fortune favors the bold.

TAO

Musashi's second rule is, "The Way is in the training." Another way to say this is, "The Way is in the practice." Both meanings point us in the direction of the inward path to the Way.

"The Way" is the English translation of the word "Tao" or "Dao." The Way is more of a philosophical path. It is not a literal way or path, complete with a set of rules and instructions to follow. This is intentional. The ancient Taoists knew that it was essential to keep the voice inside the head from becoming activated by asking all kinds of meaningless questions, and getting caught up in specific how-to's.

The Way is actually very feminine. It's the inward path. It is the Way to go deep to the place women intuitively know and understand — to our place of strength.

The Way is the Way of peace and the Way of non-action. Non-action, called "Wu Wei," is at the heart of the Way. It is meant to be attained through being receptive rather than by taking action. By being open and allowing, instead of being closed and forcing.

Non-action, though, should not be confused with being passive. Nor should it be confused with taking no action. The very act of going inward takes action and determination. To go inward in the face of anger takes decisiveness and strength. To go inward when every part of you wants to lash out in retaliation, takes control. To go inward to find your center and place of peace when everything in your world is falling apart, takes conviction. To go inward for counsel, sustenance, and renewal, takes practice.

This is the secret to your inner journey.

Kwannon, the bodhisattva of compassion, knew this secret. Musashi practiced it.

KNOW THE WAY

Musashi's third and fourth rules, "Become acquainted with every art," and "Know the Ways of all professions," aren't to be taken literally. He's not talking about learning every profession and art form. Instead, he is talking about knowing the essence, the spirit, and the core of everything. He is talking about looking beneath the surface to something deeper, more profound, and more fundamental in nature — to the heart of compassion.

Musashi's third and fourth rules move you into your Inner Samurai's place of compassion — into the heart of Kwannon. Into the heart of all.

This is the place where our Inner Samurai dwells — the place of open-heartedness. Here, the lotus flower is in full bloom. From this place, your Inner Samurai takes action — action that flows outward in love and compassion for all. Action that comes from a place of expansion, not contraction. From a place of inclusion, not exclusion. This is a place women intuitively know — a place where having compassion for one means having compassion for all.

INNER SAMURAI DISCERNMENT

Musashi's fifth rule, "Distinguish between gain and loss in worldly matters," means to distinguish between what is beneficial and what is detrimental to you. The key to this kind of discernment is understanding that it is built upon the foundation of compassion. Discernment is the outward expression of an inward knowing, where decisions are based on taking in the whole while discerning the one.

This is the place of Inner Samurai decision making. It's a way of taking action in the world that may be new to you. This rule is based on Musashi's first four rules. It presumes you know who you are and what you want. It presupposes you have practiced going inward and getting in touch with your Inner Samurai. It considers that your inner work has brought you into direct relationship with your heart of compassion, and that action in the outer world will be taken from there.

The challenge of this rule isn't whether you will discern what is beneficial for you, but whether or not you will take action based on that knowledge. How many times have you known what was right for you yet made another choice — one that was wrong for you? How many times have you gone against your inner knowing?

How many times have you heard yourself say, "I knew I should have gone that way, done that thing, or spoken my truth?" It happens to all of us — women more than men. Why? Because women generally worry more about the opinions of others.

That's why Musashi's rule is so important for women. Being who you are and discerning what is most beneficial to you is what tapping into your Inner Samurai is all about.

Intuition, the Unsung Heroine

Musashi's sixth and seventh rules, "Develop intuitive judgment and understanding for everything," and "Perceive those things that cannot be seen" go nicely together. Here, Musashi is talking about developing your intuition. Although intuition is discussed more fully in chapter seven of this book, it is helpful now for you to know that the word *intuition* comes from the Latin word *intueri*, meaning, "to look within."

In Japan, intuition is known as "stomach art." As such, it is considered an art form. The only thing we have similar to stomach art in the West is what many would call a "gut reaction" or "gut feeling." I'm sure you've heard people say, "I'm just going with my gut on this one." Or, "I have a gut feeling about this." When people say these things, they are letting you know that they are getting information from a source other than their thinking mind. We've all heard stories about people who decided not to get on a plane flight at the last minute because they just had a gut feeling that something terrible was going to happen — and they were right.

Musashi's sixth rule is instructing us to go inward and rely on our inner knowing, our Inner Samurai, when making decisions and judgments. Pay attention to your Inner Samurai. Value it. Your intuition is strengthened when you go inward and listen to what your Inner Samurai is saying. Act on your intuition. Trust it.

Pay Attention and be Useful

Musashi's last two rules go together, too: "Pay attention even to trifles," and "Do nothing that is of no use." Paying attention to trifles is having an eye for detail — though not so much detail that you get lost in it and end up making it a useless pursuit.

In today's fast-paced world, it is very easy for us to gloss over details, go on autopilot, and multi-task several things at once. Musashi's last two rules don't recommend that as a way of life. He reminds us to slow down, take time, and pay attention to the details. This is great advice for men and women alike. It is particularly helpful for women, since we seem to be masters of keeping multiple plates up in the air.

"Yeah, but," I can hear you saying, "How do I slow down long enough to notice the details?" Musashi's final rule provides that answer: "Do nothing that is of no use." How many meaningless things do you do in a day? How many things on your current "to do" list are truly meaningful and don't "need" to be done?

Think about it. Is the laundry of use? How about grocery shopping? What about sending that email, updating your website, having lunch with your colleague, or putting together that sales spreadsheet? What about picking up your kids, going to the gym, watching TV, or complaining about your spouse? What about those last-minute things you just have to get done before you go to bed or that chiropractic appointment you've been meaning to make?

By determining what is of use and paying attention to detail, your day will naturally slow down. You will feel less stressed and more focused. You will enjoy life more.

And so, through Musashi's last two rules, we come full circle. We return to the outer samurai world. Musashi has shown us the path inward, reminded us that compassion is at the heart of our Inner Samurai, and finally, led us back to our outer world to practice mindfulness and usefulness, day-to-day, moment-to-moment.

NOTES FROM YOUR INNER SAMURAI

Those who have no compassion have no wisdom. Knowledge, yes; cleverness, maybe; wisdom, no. A clever mind is not a heart. Knowledge doesn't really care. Wisdom does.

— The Tao of Pooh

Consider reading *The Book of Five Rings*. Already read the book and found it to be a bit dry for your taste? Well, now that you know what wonderful hidden gems can be discovered beneath the surface, perhaps you'll read it again.

Find out more about the bodhisattva Guan Yin (Kwannon). If this is the first time you've ever heard of her, get to know this beautiful, white-robed woman of compassion.

Be honest about who you are and what you really want. Then let the important people in your life get to know you. Communicate with them. Share your thoughts, ideas, and dreams.

Practice the Way. Make the Way your path. Follow the Way to your heart of compassion.

- Let right action be inspired action — action arising from the inside out.

- Practice stomach art.

- Pay attention to all things. Take delight in detail.

- Be of good use.

Part II

The Accidental Pren-her Way

Chapter 5

DOING WHAT YOU LOVE
MULTIPLE-STREAMS-OF-PASSION

*Great dancers aren't great because of their technique;
they are great because of their passion.*

— Martha Graham

Are you someone who has many interests? Do you like to read and write, fix and invent, design projects and start businesses, and many other things, all at once? Do you feel limited by the word "or," uncomfortable when you need to narrow down choices, and absolutely revolted by the command to "pick one?" Is "and" your favorite word?

If so, welcome to the world of what I affectionately call "multiple-streams-of-passion people"— people with multiple interests, multiple passions, and lots of passionate possibilities. If you are a multiple-streams-of-passion person, you love to do it all. You thrive on choice. You like to beat your own drum and follow your own direction. You like the flexibility and freedom of going from one thing to the next.

This would be all well and good except for one thing: You haven't learned how to harness the power of your passion to produce a steady flow of income. As a result, you flounder in careers, languish in professions, and fail at businesses.

A multiple-streams-of-passion person is often labeled, none too kindly, as a jack-of-all-trades, master of none. Does this sound familiar? Have you ever been criticized for pursuing too many directions at once? Have you ever been misunderstood regarding why you are having such a hard time making a decision or choosing a direction? Do people see you as unable to make up your mind? How many times have you felt beaten down, exhausted, and completely overwhelmed because of this? Have you gotten to the point of giving up, choosing not to do anything at all, and feeling like a complete failure for doing so?

GENERALIST, NOT SPECIALIST

If so, chances are, you are a generalist. My client Tina was just like that. She had just turned 40 when she came to me, and she felt pretty beaten down. Her résumé was all over the place because she had switched jobs so frequently. She had a lot of training in seemingly unrelated disciplines because she was so darn fascinated by so much. She was, as she called herself, the "life of the party" until it came to talking about what she did for a living. That's when she would falter. While other people around her talked excitedly about their work, Tina only had ideas, interests, and passions that she was pursuing — not an actual career she could talk about.

It seemed like what she did for a living switched every couple of years. Three years prior, Tina was so excited about Feng Shui that she took the time to become a Certified Feng Shui Practitioner. Just as she got serious about starting up her Feng Shui business, her attention was diverted by landscape design. Her boyfriend, exasperated by what he saw as yet another tangential career change, threw his hands in the air, saying, "Can't you just stick to one thing for awhile? Can't you just be normal?"

Tina felt deflated. Her bubble had been burst. She really liked Feng Shui and even saw how getting a degree in architectural design would strengthen and complement her Feng Shui business, though her boyfriend didn't want to hear anything about it. "The problem with you is, you just can't focus," he declared. "You are so easily distracted by the next great thing that comes along. Why do you always think the grass is greener on the other side?"

That's when Tina came to me. She thought she needed help getting her Feng Shui business up and running. Maybe, she thought, she would get a business plan under her belt, a five-year strategic plan designed, and marketing material developed. Tina wasn't afraid to get to work, that's for sure. The problem was, Tina wasn't being driven by passion. She was being driven by a combination of guilt, fear, and imminent failure.

LET'S TALK

That's the first thing I said to Tina on our third coaching session.

"Okay," she said, ready to do anything.

"Is starting up a Feng Shui business what you really want to do?"

"Yes, of course!"

"So, what about architectural design? Where does that fit in? And what about your passion for Ikebana (Japanese Floral Design)?"

"Oh, yes," she breathed with rapture. "I love Ikebana. I was thinking about taking a class in it this fall."

"And . . . architectural design?" I prompted.

"Well, yes, it would be really great if I did that, too."

"So, which is it that you want to do first?"

"Definitely the Feng Shui business. No, wait, I think I had better get some architectural design classes under my belt first. I could go to architectural design school for a year and take Ikebana classes on the side."

"Okay, so it's settled then. You're going to go enroll for a degree in architectural design and take some Ikebana classes on the side. Sounds to me like you won't be starting up a Feng Shui business in the near future."

"Oh, no, wait! I can't do that! I love Feng Shui! I worked so hard to be certified. I have to do that!"

"*Have* to do that?

"Want to do that. 'Have to,' as in, I will die if I don't!"

Tina was caught in a classic example of what happens when a woman is facing multiple-streams-of-passion. She just doesn't know what to do. She gets overwhelmed. She tries to keep all the doors open, all the options available, and all the balls up in the air. She can't stand the thought of not doing one of the many things she loves to do. The last thing she wants is to have to choose just one.

DEVELOPING MULTIPLE-STREAMS-OF-PASSION

Doing what we love is one of the most exhilarating feelings on earth. It's like no other. It is at once sublime and invigorating. I bet you know exactly what I'm talking about! With breast to the wind, shirttails flapping, and arms outstretched, it's a ride-of-your-life feeling. Most of us have felt this feeling more than once in our lives. We know the call, like a lover to his beloved.

That's the call of passion. Passion is energy. Passion is vitality. As talk show host Oprah Winfrey says, "Passion is the power that comes from focusing on what excites you." Passion is closely linked with creativity; it is kissing cousins with intuition. Women have passion in spades. Not that men don't; it just seems that it is easier for women to tap into our passion. Yet, partly because of cultural upbringing and the society that we currently live in, passion is often overlooked or ignored.

My brother Larry and I were fortunate. We grew up in a home where passion and creativity were encouraged. Momacita was highly creative and passionate about many things. Often, when we were kids, she would pack Larry and I up in the car and just go exploring to see what we would see. Sometimes we would come back from those rides with raspberry stains on our fingers and a gallon of sun-warmed raspberries to turn into pies, jam, and war paint. Other times, we would come back with snails, salamanders, and frog eggs that we put into an old fish bowl to observe like a biology project.

Momacita was always fueling our creativity and passion by doing dozens of craft projects each year. At home, our basement was the seat of much creativity. Any number of things could and would often be going on at the same time — especially during the winter months. In one corner were the sand candles we made out of old candles. In another, were the Reid Coat of Arms my dad was carving out of wood, and the display he and Larry were putting together using all the trains and track they could find in our attic. In another corner sat the Ukrainian eggs Momacita was painstakingly detailing with wax, right alongside my tie-dye shirt and pants collection that I had hopes of selling at a Grateful Dead concert. (Yeah right, like my parents were really going to let me do that!) Regardless of the practicality of anything, our parents encouraged and honored creativity.

They recognized the focus and excitement that comes from being in the flow of passion. They could see it in their children's eyes — eyes that danced with delight at each new creation. They could hear it in our voices when we figured out a cool way to do something. We saw passion in our Dad's eyes each time we visited a Confederate Battlefield or the Washington D.C. monuments. We saw it in our Momacita's eyes when she would come home with some fascinating object she had discovered at an estate sale. Larry and I experienced it together when we would test the limits of our canoeing ability in Class III waters. And we knew it separately with the rockets that Larry built and launched, and Beethoven's *Sonata Pathétique* that I finally mastered.

WORKING WITH, NOT AGAINST, YOUR MULTIPLE-STREAMS-OF-PASSION

Learning how to work with your multiple-streams-of-passion is imperative if you intend to have any financial stability or success. Moreover, it all starts with the appreciation and understanding of the creative process.

Creativity is being able to generate new ideas, concepts, and ways of solving problems from an invigoratingly fresh perspective. Creative people are bright, curious, and inquisitive. They are good at coming up with lots of ideas. For women, that often means coming up with multiple ideas at the same time. Sometimes those ideas stem from the same passion. Very often, though, they are completely divergent passions that seem *to others* not to have any connecting thread at all. If this describes you, you may have noticed that other people may not know how you got from Point A to B, but you know.

How many times have you been on the phone with your girlfriend when, out of the blue, she says something like, "Oh, yeah, that reminds me, I was out with Joan and her husband the other night and thought of a way that you could incorporate that new radio segment you talked about last week into your website. Let me tell you about it." Immediately, the conversation flips on a dime and you are off, running in a completely different direction. That's what the creative process is like.

CREATIVITY AND THE RIGHT BRAIN

Creativity is associated with the right-side hemisphere of the brain. This is the intuitive, artistic, expressive side of the brain. This is the side where "thinking" and learning is done by visualizing pictures; doing is done from a kinesthetic, hands on approach; and listening is quickly translated into images. Right-brain thinkers don't like to go from Point A to B, and don't often like listening to or following directions. They scan quickly and figure out what to do without reading details.

Right-brain thinkers like associative thinking. Called non-linear thinking, this seemingly random association of ideas, thoughts, and words makes perfect sense to right-brainers and fortuitously links them in creative and exciting ways to perfect solutions, people, and places. This kind of thinking comes naturally to people with multiple-streams-of-passion, though it has caused many a confused listener to scratch her head and say "What? Where did that come from?"

Because right-brain thinkers see and quickly comprehend the big picture, they often don't like to be bogged down with sequential processes. That's because right-brain thinkers like patterns (such as pattern recognition in music), not individual pieces. That's why right-brainers are terrible at putting together a traditional business plan, preferring instead, to put together One Page Business Plans®. Since working with creative entrepreneurial women, I've learned the hard way that the fastest way to shut down a multiple-streams-of-passion person is to insist on doing a traditional business plan. Today, I only do One Page Business Plans®, and this has made a crucial difference in their success.

There's one thing to keep in mind when talking about right — and left-brain thinking — each of us has a marvelous corpus callosum. With the exception of those who have had surgery or injury, the corpus callosum connects the right and left hemispheres of the brain, keeping the two hemispheres in constant communication with each other. In addition, the corpus callosum is typically larger in women, thus speculating that women's right and left brains are in greater communication with each other.

As Tina and I progressed together, it became clear that Tina was also strong in her left-side hemisphere thinking. The analytical part of her could and actually enjoyed looking at things and examining them from every direction. She could also be objective and had the ability to see the parts as well as the whole in any idea she was considering.

THE ADVANTAGES OF WHOLE BRAIN THINKING

Tina is what I would call more of a whole-brain thinker. She is someone who has the ability to be both right-brain creative and left-brain logical. Right-brainers, if also strong in their left-brain hemisphere thinking, make fantastic entrepreneurs. So do left brainers, if also strong in their creative, right-brain thinking. Both types have abilities to generate and embrace new ideas, while being able to put a plan into action.

Put simply, the more whole brain thinking you do, the easier it will be for you to make the seemingly impossible, possible. It will be easier for you to take your fantastic array and collection of ideas and turn them into multiple-streams-of-passion that are profitable, sustainable, and exceedingly rewarding. The more whole brain thinking you can develop (and you *can* strengthen whichever side of your brain is less dominant), the less likely it will be that you will find yourself hopelessly trapped on the merry-go-round of one creative idea after another, never able to get off.

This is the key to turning your multiple-streams-of-passion into a viable whole. This is the way Tina turned her boyfriend Karl around from being an exasperated, critical doomsayer into an onboard, supportive fan.

Assuming that you are not still trying to make up your mind about what you are going to do when you grow up, or are depressed and not able to focus on any one thing for long, or have Adult Attention Deficit Disorder and are easily distracted, then consider that you might be someone with multiple-streams-of-passion. Consider that all you might need is a little strengthening in your non-dominant brain hemisphere, some creative guidance as to how to turn your passions into profits, and support in making that happen.

If you are someone who is clinically depressed or has been diagnosed with Adult ADD, it's a little harder to distinguish the difference between multiple-streams-of-passion and having difficulty focusing or being easily distracted. It is estimated that more than eight million adults may have Adult ADD, and many don't realize it. If you are depressed or have Adult ADD, you may need other professional support in addition to creative guidance and support from a coach or consultant.

TAKE YOUR INSPIRATION FROM THE POLYMATHS

A polymath (pah'-lee-math) is, simply put, a multiple scholar — someone with encyclopedic, broad, and varied knowledge or learning in several different fields of study. During the Renaissance period (1450-1600), it was not all that unusual to make the pursuit of becoming a polymath one's life ambition. Scholars, especially in Europe, were given free reign to explore the world around them and often studied astronomy, biology, natural history, literature, art, music, and whatever else took their fancy. They felt free to study across disciplines and collaborate with others in different fields, and they did so with ease and regularity.

Scholars, at that time, knew that there was an inherent value in being polymathic. However, the Industrial Revolution in Great Britain during the 18th century, and later in America and Germany in the 19th century, changed all that. Specialization became the prized commodity. If you were specialized in any given field, it implied great knowledge in that field and recognition was awarded with authority. By the mid-19th century, specialization was seen as far more desirable than polymathy.

Happily, though, for those who are multiple-streams-of-passion people, the pendulum has begun its movement back to a more centered position. With the dissolution of large corporations and the rise of information and communications technology, specialization in just one field is being seen as more of a hindrance than a help. Specialization is becoming a behemoth, while polymath-esque thinking is being looked at with more appreciation.

Though it is still not as openly encouraged as it was in the Renaissance Era, there is a growing trend today for people to be more polymathic in their thinking and being. Whether called the new "Renaissance men and women" of the 21st century, "Universal geniuses," "whiz kids," or "geeks," being a polymath, or even just thinking like one, is coming into favor and being seen, once again, as a tremendous attribute. In fact, polymathy is actually gaining in stature and prominence as more and more people are figuring out how to turn their multiple-streams-of-passion into sustainable profits.

Leonardo da Vinci is one of the most famous polymaths. He was a scientist, mathematician, engineer, inventor, anatomist, painter, sculptor, architect, musician, and writer.

Before him was Claudius Ptolemy who was a Greek mathematician, geographer, astronomer, and astrologer.

Hildegard of Bingen, a German abbess, was recognized as an artist, author, counselor, dramatist, linguist, natural historian, philosopher, physician, poet, political consultant, visionary, and composer.

Gottfried Leibniz made significant contributions in physics, logic, history, librarianship, philosophy, and theology, while also working on ideal languages, mechanical clocks, and mining machinery.

Thomas Jefferson achieved distinction as a horticulturist, statesman, architect, archaeologist, paleontologist, author, inventor, founder of the University of Virginia, and third President of The United States of America.

Johann Wolfgang von Goethe was a polymath of letters: he was a poet, critic, playwright, and novelist.

Mary Somerville was the most celebrated woman scientist of her time. She wrote on astronomy, mathematics, physics, chemistry, mineralogy, and geology.

Alexander Borodin was a chemist and composer, conducted scientific research, and campaigned for women to be allowed to study medicine.

Jane Addams won the Nobel Peace Prize and was a founder of the U.S. Settlement House Movement. She was known for her writing, her work with the Camp Fire Girls, and her work against child labor. She actively supported the campaign for woman suffrage and the founding of the American Civil

Liberties Union, and carried out international efforts for world peace.

Andrei Sakharov was a brilliant nuclear physicist, human rights campaigner, and fearless advocate for international understanding and world peace.

Umberto Eco is a modern polymath. He is an Italian medievalist, semiotician, philosopher, expert in pop culture, and novelist.

POLYMATHY AND THE ACCIDENTAL PREN-HER

Accidental Pren-hers know that there are no accidents. Therefore, becoming an Accidental Pren-her is not really an accident. It's about design and recognizing that design, more than anything else.

That's what Tina discovered about herself, most specifically, about her multiple-streams-of-passion. Instead of fighting against what was most natural for her by narrowing down her options and trying to make herself fit in, she began to accept herself. She began accepting the strength of her passion; the grand design of her multiple-streams-of-passion pren-hership.

It was a marvelous thing to hear the excited acceptance in her voice one day when she said "Susan, I'm ready. I'm ready to quit fighting against myself, ready to quit listening to what other people have told me about focusing in on one thing, and am open to exploring where my multiple-streams-of-passion will take me."

Over the course of the next couple of months together, we sifted out the wheat from the chaff, looking at what Tina was really passionate about, versus what she was good at doing.

Doing What You Love
Multiple-Streams-of-Passion

Ch. 5

The thing about multiple-streams-of-passion people is that they are often very good at many different things. They are so much more than jacks-of-all-trades. They are, most of the time, masters of many, with some having 25 years or more of study and research in multiple fields. Their passions may have been directed into a career at one time, and then re-directed into something else when children and family came along. They may have been very successful at one thing, reached the upper limit of what they wanted to do, and then moved on to something else. However, the pattern of direction and re-direction continued.

Finding the core passion, the one passion from which all other passions flow, is a process that Tina thoroughly enjoyed doing. Once she arrived at her top main passion, she was ready to play a game I call *Planet and Moons*.

FINDING YOUR PLANET

The purpose of the *Planet and Moons* game is to discover your one main passion: The passion that is at the center of all your other passions. So, one day I said to Tina, "Cut out 10 circles. Now, on each of those circles write the name of the 10 passions you have identified."

Tina wrote: architectural design, flower arranging, space, presentation, color, understanding the big picture, nature, Japanese storytelling, writing, and spirituality.

> "Now, clear the space in front of you and spread your circles around so none of them are touching."

85

"Okay."

"What do you see?"

"There are certain pairings that make more sense together than others, though they all become a big blur to me when I look at them together."

"I bet they do! This is what happens when multiple-streams-of-passions come together. They collide, run into, and bump each other around. That's why multi-streams people have so much difficulty making up their minds about what they want to focus on. There are so many streams competing for attention, competing for fulfillment."

"Yes, exactly!"

"Okay then. Let's get back to the pairings you can see. What naturally goes together for you?"

"Architectural design, space, presentation, and color."

"Great. Now put those together in a pile and set them off to the side."

"Do you see another pairing or grouping in the remaining circles?" I continued.

"Ummm . . . okay. I can see how Japanese storytelling and flower arranging can go together; they both tell stories."

"Perfect! Place those two off to another side and look at the remaining three. Do you see any grouping or pairing there?"

"Yes. Spirituality and understanding the big picture go together. Though, I just don't see writing fitting in anywhere."

> "That's fine. Place the two that go together off to another side and set writing off by itself."
>
> "Wait," she stopped me. "Now I can see how writing can go with my Japanese storytelling and flower arranging group."
>
> "Super! Put it there. So, now we have three groups. Do you still feel good about your groupings?"
>
> "Yes!"

Together, Tina and I carefully examined each of her groups to determine which group stood out the strongest for her, and to determine which circle within each group was most dominant. In the end, she selected three circles: flower arranging, architectural design, and spiritual. These became Tina's three main "planets."

> "Okay, Tina, your assignment for next week is to decide which of these three planets is your central planet. This will be the planet that belongs in the center of your paper, the planet that is exerting the greatest gravitational pull on all the surrounding planets, which we will call 'moons.' Over the course of this week, I want you to determine your planet and moons."

When Tina came back, she had identified flower arranging as her main planet. However, she was having a lot of resistance to this because she was certain she could not make any money at being a flower arranger, nor did she really want to. In fact, she was a bit panicked about how this exercise had turned out for her, secretly hoping that architectural design would show up as the main planet so that she would be justified in going off and getting her architectural design degree. Try as she might, though, every time she put her architectural design circle in the middle, she felt a clear *no* pulse from her inner knower, her Inner Samurai.

> "Tell me more about what you mean when you say flower arranging. What kind of flowers? What kind of arrangements?"
>
> "Flower arranging to me is more than just putting flowers in a vase. You know, like you see from most florists. It's more about the placement of certain flowers in relationship to certain linear aspects. I also don't like to use too many flowers, preferring to keep things simple, with clean lines. The flower arrangement isn't just about the flowers. It's about vase selection, which way the stems are going, and structure. I like structure. In the end, it's about the complete picture that it all makes together."

That sounded a lot like the Ikebana art of flower arranging, which she had first talked about at the beginning of our coaching sessions.

> I asked, "Tina, if we scratched out 'flower arranging' and wrote 'Ikebana', does that resonate more closely to what you mean by flower arranging?"
>
> "Yes!" she exclaimed. "And, with Ikebana in the center, I can see how some of my other moons can be arranged to flow around it in a more exciting and dynamic way."
>
> "So, Tina, let's take this one step further. What was your impetus behind becoming a Certified Feng Shui Practitioner? I know you put a lot of time and attention into getting certified. What do you think that was about for you?"

"It was about finding myself."

"Finding yourself?" I asked, a little perplexed by that response. "Tell me more about that."

"I discovered so much about me during my training and certification process that I didn't know before. For instance, I found out how important space and presentation are to me. How color, architectural design, and the way they all go together in a home, garden, or common area is rather like a spiritual experience for me. I also found out I like detail. I like to be specific. I like to be precise. Feng Shui was the one thing that combined all my passions into a complete whole."

"Makes sense to me. So, how come you don't have a Feng Shui circle, then?"

"Well, because no one was really supportive of me as I went through the program. Here I was all excited, coming into my friends' and family's homes adding things, re-arranging things, moving things around, and it really wasn't well received. They mostly just laughed and teased, 'Yeah, right; I can feel how this makes a difference in my energy.' So I just stopped."

Now we had come to the crux of the matter. Tina was trying, once again, to re-direct her passion. To mold it into something else that was going to be more acceptable to the people around her. She was trying to be other than who she was.

Has that ever happened to you? I know it's something I've often done. It's an uncomfortable, restrictive, hopeless feeling, isn't it? As if nothing's ever good enough. Tina was experiencing that, too.

USING THE POLYMATHIC MODEL AS YOUR GUIDE

If you were living in the Renaissance Era (and you were a man, of course), it would be much easier for you to follow your multiple-streams-of-passion. Inspired by your Inner Samurai and encouraged by the society and culture around you, you'd be strolling in the King's garden, surrounded by roses.

Well, you deserve to be in the King's garden now! Passion is the Accidental Pren-her way. Multiple-streams-of-passion is the Tao of the polymath. Left alone, undisturbed or mitigated by others, all streams find their way to the ocean. So does a polymath. So will you.

Women are polymathic by nature. They view their lives from a whole-istic viewpoint. They don't break their lives down into separate pieces. Women create lives — not life parts. Our ability to unite seemingly contrasting parts into a whole is one of our greatest strengths.

This ability is also one of the earmarks of the polymath. Besides the ability to see previously incongruent ideas and to create new relationships between disparate data sets, polymaths are a great inspiration for multiple-streams-of-passion people.

Tina found the polymath model very helpful. Whenever she got frustrated and wanted to throw in the towel, she reminded herself of the polymathic men and women who had gone before her, and that inspired her to move along, too. Here's what she kept in mind:

1. Polymaths are terminally curious.

It's okay to be curious.

2. Polymaths read widely in and move freely across the boundaries of divergent and not always complementary disciplines. This natural tendency is often what brings about the formulation of brilliant discoveries, new applications, and luminous collaborations.

   I will let my Inner Samurai guide me to what's next, knowing that it will all be connected in the end.

3. Polymaths have the ability to focus powerfully on a given topic for long periods — meaning, for as long as necessary to learn what they need to know. Then they move on. They don't focus on one thing to the exclusion of everything else. Rather, their focus on each thing is a stepping-stone to the next great thing they will explore.

   This doesn't mean I have to finish everything. It just means that I need to stay the course long enough to plumb everything about a topic that I am passionate about knowing or doing.

4. Polymaths are fantastic synthesizers.

   Blending, combining, amalgamating, and integrating are what I do well.

5. Polymaths excel at generating ideas. They think conceptually first.

   I naturally think big-to-small, general-to-specific, and infinite-to-finite. I will allow myself to unfold effortlessly in this manner.

What happened to Tina? I am pleased to announce that after a year of working together, Tina launched her Feng Shui business. And, through her business, all the rest of her passions now flow. She couldn't be happier (neither could her boyfriend, now fiancé). Tina's day is varied, and, through the course of a week, she gets to focus on some aspect of each of her moons. Tina did decide to take a couple of classes in Ikebana and now sells customized Ikebana arrangements as complementary products in her Feng Shui business. Instead of going back to school and getting a degree in architectural design, she is talking with prospective partners who have strengths in architectural design about coming into her business.

Now, when someone exasperatedly throws his or her hands up in the air and says, "I have no idea how you got from there to here," Tina just smiles sweetly and says, "I'm brilliant!"

Notes from Your Inner Samurai

Everything you need you already have. You are complete right now; you are a whole, total person, not an apprentice person on the way to someplace else. Your completeness must be understood by you and experienced in your thoughts as your own personal reality.

— Beverly Sills

- Learn to think favorably about your particular way of doing things.

- Understand that it won't take long, once you have discovered your primary passion, to flow all your other passions through it to a sustainable, profitable whole.

- There's nothing wrong with you. Put down the self-help books and pick up autobiographies and biographies of famous polymaths to inspirit and inspire you.

- Make no apology and offer no excuse for how you have gotten from Point A to B. Take your lead from Tina. When asked, simply throw your head back, laugh delightedly, and say, "I'm brilliant!"

- Stop beating yourself up for going in circles. Instead, take the lead in finding out what your primary passion is, then flow everything in that direction.

History books don't list many women polymaths. Make history. Or, I should say, herstory.

Trust yourself. Listen to your Inner Samurai. She will never lead you astray, do you wrong, or leave you hanging. She always has your highest good and greatest wellbeing at heart. True, it may not make much sense to you today, but you know how that is: It will tomorrow.

Chapter 6

THE HERO'S JOURNEY
A HEROINE'S APPROACH

It is our choices . . . that show what we truly are, far more than our abilities.

— J.K. Rowling

A bootstrap, in the traditional use of the word, is a loop attached to the back or sides of a boot to assist the wearer in pulling it on. The purpose of having bootstraps is to allow the wearer to be entirely self-sufficient, making the boot easier to get into. This works very well for boots. Not always so well when starting up your own business.

By the 19th century, the phrase, "to pull oneself up by the bootstraps," had become an adage, an emblem of the blood-sweat-and-tears spirit that was sweeping across the land. Americans moved westward to stake their claim in vast acres of land and moved even further West during the California Gold Rush of 1849. There was an element of pride inherent in carving out a place for yourself in the New World. This same spirit propelled us into the

20th century. Today, however, with the wide use of global information and communications technology, the bootstrap spirit that thrust us into the 20th century has waned.

Like Avalon, that magical land of Arthurian legend that faded into the mists, so too is bootstrapping fading into myth. Bootstrapping is becoming passé. The term is losing its meaning in the lexicon of today's LinkedIn or Facebook professional. There is no longer any need to stake a claim in the small business world all by yourself. There are plenty of people to help you out. Plenty of people who are eager to do so. We are here to help each other. We are here to pool resources, brainstorm ideas, and encourage each other on the road to success.

Today's business professionals and entrepreneurs are not here to reinvent the wheel each and every time they do something new. We're all here to communicate, share, expand, and move forward together toward better and greater things. Those who think otherwise may as well be stuck in a world of distrust populated with beady-eyed Snidely Whiplash characters. Those who hold close the secrets of their success, telling no one — or charging exorbitant sums of money in order to reveal those secrets — do not understand the world as it is unfolding today.

They do not understand that our society, culture, and world have changed. Today, holding on to secrets is futile. Forcing others to make the same mistakes we've made, again and again, is pointless. What lesson is to be learned by doing things the hard way — the old bootstrap way?

None. Instead, I'm here to tell you that the journey to be walked, the adventure to be had, will occur with the help of your friends, guides, and trusted professionals.

Know that you will and must walk parts of this journey alone. Fortunately, however, you will walk the majority of it with others. This is The Heroine's Journey. The journey that each one of us takes from Accidental Pren-her to entrepreneurial woman.

THE HERO'S JOURNEY — FOR WOMEN, TOO

The Hero's Journey is a *monomyth* — a description of a basic pattern found in many narratives from around the world. Joseph Campbell, though not the first to use it, was the first to popularize it. Campbell, a 20th century American mythology professor and writer best known for his work in the fields of comparative mythology and comparative religion, borrowed the idea of the Hero's Journey from Irish author James Joyce. His book, *The Hero with a Thousand Faces,* first talks about the concept of the Hero's Journey as a monomyth. Later, *The Hero's Journey: The World of Joseph Campbell* expounds upon that myth.

Through his research, Campbell discovered that the Hero's Journey is a myth of such great importance that it is included in all of the major world cultures. These myths, with their mythological and religious heroes (Osiris, Prometheus, Moses, Buddha, and Christ, to name a few), have survived for thousands of years and all share the same fundamental structure. Although the stages or steps along the journey vary in number, the three main aspects of the Hero's Journey remain the same.

These three aspects — Departure, Initiation, and Return — constitute the journey from Accidental Pren-her to entrepreneurial women. It's immensely helpful to understand the Hero's — or, in this case, the Heroine's — Journey, so you can identify where you are along the path and not get lost or give up along the way. As a result, you will become a powerful and effective agent for your own transformation. What's more, you will discover that change, while certainly life altering, can also be life affirming, life enhancing, and oh so satisfying.

DEPARTURE

The adventure begins when the heroine receives a call to action. The call to action, according to Campbell, usually comes when "a blunder — apparently the merest chance — reveals an unsuspected world, and the individual is drawn into a relationship with forces that are not rightly understood."[1] This activating event is often seen as a threat to the peace of the individual or the community. It is often brought on by another person, an outside event, or a spiritual occurrence.

If you are someone who has been downsized from the corporate world, has lost your job, or has quit simply because you've had enough of working for someone else, then this is your activating event. If your children have recently left home or you are newly divorced, this is also an activating event.

The spiritual experience discussed in chapters one and three of this book was my call to action. What was yours? Maybe it was the death of a loved one. Perhaps you've come into some money. Maybe you've had a near-miss accident. Whatever event it was, it became your heralded call for change: A call to action.

Once the call is received, the heroine has a choice — to accept or decline. There is always that choice. No one is ever forced to go on a Heroine's Journey. This is one of those times when the decision is a singular decision. It is up to you to decide if you are going to heed the call to action or not. If you say *yes*, your world will change. If you say *no*, it will still change, though in a different way. Campbell explains, "Refusal of the summons converts the adventure into its negative. Walled in boredom, hard work, or 'culture,' the subject loses the power of significant affirmative action and becomes a victim to be saved."[2]

For those who are contemplating becoming a small business owner, this is the time when you decide if you will or will not venture forth; if you will or will not take your first steps toward entrepreneurship. Will you heed the call or become a victim to be saved? No matter what your decision, the fact remains, *something unexpected has happened in your life that is shaping who you are and what you do today.* You can't go back. You can never go back to the time before the call. The question is: Will you go on?

Many of us don't. However, the few who do are changed forever. The Heroine's Journey shapes us, transforms us, and spits us out whole with a fire in our bellies and a deeper inner knowing that we've never had before — an Inner Samurai knowing.

INITIATION

After the heroine has accepted the call and sets off down the road, she must cross the threshold between the world she is familiar with and the unknown world. This is the heroine's road of trials. This is the time when she is tested; where she is honed and strengthened by the journey.

Sounds rather daunting, doesn't it? Well, there is good news. We don't travel this part of the journey alone. Many allies and friends will walk with us. Some known, some unknown. Some will protect us. Others will guide us. Still others will be older and wiser to provide sound counsel and sage advice. Those we meet will provide us with the tools and insights for the adventure ahead. This is the part of the journey where we go it *together*. Where synchronistic events, seemingly chance encounters, and the most unexpectedly helpful guides come to assist us and walk with us along our way.

Remember the scene in the movie version of *The Fellowship of the Ring*[3] when Gandalf tells Frodo that he is no longer safe in the Shire, that the ring Bilbo has left him is the One Ring, the ring being sought after by the Dark Lord Sauron? This is the moment of Frodo's call to action. He and his beloved Shire are threatened if he stays. He accepts the call to take the One Ring to Rivendell, and at that moment Sam appears to walk by his side, to accompany him, no matter what.

Together they set off on their great adventure. Everything is going along just fine until Sam suddenly stops at the edge of a cornfield. Frodo keeps walking ahead and hasn't noticed for a few seconds that Sam is no longer with him. When he does, he turns back and sees Sam looking down at the ground in front of him.

"What is it, Sam?" Frodo asks.

"This is it. If I take one more step, it will be the farthest from home I have ever been."

This is what the experience of crossing the threshold between what you know and what you don't know is like. This is the place between worlds. Between what is familiar and what is not. No matter how excited you may be on our journey, that place where you cross over can stop you in your tracks. You don't know what lies ahead. You are in new, uncharted territory.

This is the place where many small business owners get hung up. It's where they are foiled; where they become fearful of moving on.

What do you call this place? I've heard it called "sitting on the fence." Others say this is the place where the "rubber meets the road." What's the experience like? One client of mine described it as the feeling of straddling two planets with one foot on Earth and the other on Mars. Another client said she felt like she was straddling the Grand Canyon with one foot on the north side and the other on the south. Both felt what Sam felt — a coming to the end of what is known and understood.

Who's Walking Beside You?

This is why we are sent friends, allies, and guides to accompany us on this part of the journey. To go it alone would be unbearable. Companionship makes it bearable, even enjoyable. Those who share the journey with us are witnesses to our initiation. They are there to support us as we face our trials and celebrate with us as we achieve victories. Frodo had his hobbit friends, Pippin, Merry, and Sam. Later, Strider (the older, more experienced adventurer) came along, and, of course, there had always been Gandalf (the wise one). Then, as Frodo was further tested, the elf Arwen and her father, Lord Elrond of Rivendell, came to Frodo's assistance.

On the road to small business start-up, it's nice to know that you don't have to go it alone — you don't have to bootstrap it. There will be friends, allies, and guides to walk beside you and help you along your way.

Take a moment and think of those you already have by your side. Who's walking beside you right now? Next, think about others who could be helpful further down the road. Is there anyone you feel nudged from within, from your Inner Samurai, to turn to or seek counsel from? Consider getting in touch with them. Tell them of your start-up plans. Consider inviting them to join in your Heroine's Journey. My guess is they will be delighted to do so. After all, *your* journey will be their journey. We are all on this journey, together.

RETURN

The last part of the Heroine's Journey is the return home. Before returning home, however, there is usually some sacrifice required — something the heroine must willingly leave behind. Quite often, it is some aspect of the heroine's ego that must be sacrificed; other times it is something physical.

Regardless, the sacrifice is always some part of us that needs to be transformed. Some part of us that is holding us back from becoming who we are and from achieving what we most desire.

When I was a teenager, I remember reading *Hinds' Feet on High Places* by English author Hannah Hurnard. This beautifully written allegorical book had a great impact on me. It was my first encounter with the feminine version of The Hero's Journey. It is the story of a young woman named Much Afraid and her spiritual journey away from her Fearing Family and into the High Places of the Shepherd, accompanied by her two companions, Sorrow and Suffering.

Together the young heroine and her allies pass through many dangers and fears as they mount to the High Places. One by one, Much Afraid faces and overcomes her doubts, turning her weaknesses into strengths and her fears into faith. At the top, she is required to sacrifice something very dear to her — her heart. And when she does, she is transformed, given a new name, and returned to the valley with new awareness and a deep knowing. She returns with gladness in her step, a smile on her face, and a new willingness to be of service to humankind.

THE START-UP JOURNEY

This is the kind of transformation that takes place along the Heroine's Journey. The gift received — or the boon, as Joseph Campbell calls it — is always an item or a new awareness that will benefit society or improve the world. Starting a business would certainly qualify as a Heroine's Journey. I tell my clients all the time that starting up a business is not really about starting up a business. "Huh?" they say. "It's about personal transformation," I qualify. "Personal transformation disguised as a small business start up. Get ready for a journey."

Most of my clients don't know they have begun their journey until they ask, "What is it that I have to offer to the world? What do I have that is so special?" When they ask these kinds of questions, I know they are walking the road of trials. The call has been heard. The departure made. Now they are facing the place where the old world self has ended and the new world self has begun. The questions that they ask at this point will shape the new world self they are becoming. The metamorphosis has begun.

What's It Like?

Starting a business from scratch is intensely creative, exciting, and adventurous. My clients speak of it as one of the most rewarding things they have ever done. Some of my clients have found it so rewarding that they have gone on to start up other businesses!

Of course, the most challenging business to begin is the first one. Starting up something new scares many people. First times are often like that. Think of anything big you did for the first time. Were you scared? Maybe a little scared mixed with a sense of adventure? Was it your first bike ride, your first date, your first day of college? That's the way it is with all big firsts. Whether it be your first kiss, your first job, or your first child, big firsts are distinguishable by their mixture of excitement and fear.

If you can think of starting up as the first step along the Heroine's Journey, your journey can then be viewed as an adventure — a first-time adventure.

Keep in mind that once you have gone out there, faced your fears, collected your boon, and returned to offer it to the world in your own unique way, your "first-time experience" is over. You are then free to go out there and back again — and again, and again. Each time with less fear, greater knowing, and more sureness of outcome.

Along the Start-up Journey, my clients ask five basic questions:

1. Is my idea good enough?
2. How do I obtain the money to start up?
3. Can I run a successful business and still have a life?
4. Do I have the necessary education and experience to do this?
5. What if I fail?

Is My Idea Good Enough?

That's a great first question along the Start-up Journey. My experience after working with hundreds of clients is that if you are serious about starting-up a business, the chances are your idea is good enough. Keep in mind the idea that you start out with will often be refined, reshaped, and re-envisioned along the journey.

By the time you have reached the place where you are thinking of starting up a business, you have likely accumulated one heck of a lot of life experience. You have acquired general information and developed expertise in one or more areas that is unique and specific to you. Unique and specific *only* to you. While you may share similar strengths and traits with others, in the final analysis, there is only one you. You have lived a life like no other. You have a viewpoint that is distinct unto you. And here's the best part: The world wants to see what you have to offer and hear what you have to say!

Be willing to go down the road of trials, and be open to have your initial ideas reshaped and reformed. That's the only way to find out, for sure, what is uniquely yours. It's the only way to uncover the jewel, to discover your niche, and to know what your unique signature in the world will be.

Rosemary started off sure that she wanted to be a relationship coach. After her Start-up Journey, she now owns a small business teaching women how to make money flipping houses. (Perhaps you've seen those shows on TV where people take old, dilapidated homes and refurbish them to sell for a nice profit.)

Helena started off thinking she wanted to open her own business as a piano tuner. It seemed a logical step for her since she is an accomplished pianist and has perfect pitch. After her Start-up Journey, she became a freelance critic writing music reviews for newspapers, magazines, and playbills. As a bonus, she always has the best seats in the house wherever she attends symphony, opera, or chorus performances.

Take this part in: *It's impossible to know completely at the start of the journey whether your initial idea is good enough.* You simply must go down the road, allow your idea to be tested, and see what comes out at the end. Yet, if you are open to the journey, if you can allow the process to unfold naturally and stay the course, you will receive your boon. Then you will be able to answer your question, "Is my idea good enough?"

How Do I Obtain the Money to Start Up?

Part of the bootstrap myth is that most people believe the only way to fund a start-up is through angel investors or venture capitalists. That was never true in the past, and it isn't true today. Yes, some opportunities require too much capital for self-funding, but certainly not all.

When considering the difference between funding your start-up yourself or funding it with other people's money, consider this: When an outsider makes a large investment in your business, they usually want a say in how their money is going to be used. This is the same for family and friends who invest in your business, as well as strangers. This is why I encourage my clients to get creative and find a way to fund their start-ups themselves, at least at first, until they have completed the Start-up Journey. That way, they are in complete control of their discoveries and won't be spending a lot of time chasing money or answering to other people's expectations.

Another advantage to using your own capital to start your business is that you get to keep a much bigger piece of the pie in the end. Don't forget that spending your own money lights a certain fire under your feet to get things going more quickly, and it naturally encourages financial discipline. It also inspires you toward becoming profitable sooner.

The sky's the limit as to how you can creatively get funding for your Start-up Journey. Some of my clients take out a second mortgage on their home. Others think this would be a great reason to use their low interest home equity line of credit. Still others go through their home or apartment from top to bottom, gather together with their neighbors, put up signs around their community, and hold one massive yard sale.

Tina didn't have much money in savings when she began her Start-up Journey. She was worried about tapping into her savings and not having a cushion. Seeing the advantages to funding the initial phase of her start-up with her own capital, Tina became creative. She rented an extra bedroom in her house to a graduate student who had family he visited in another part of the state on weekends. The arrangement worked out great for them both.

Lori had just come back from a year traveling the world when she decided to explore a great idea she had. Out of work and with not much left over from her traveling money, Lori decided to lock her car in the garage and take a part-time job in a small bookstore near her, rather than take a loan out to fund the initial stage of her start-up. This way she could bike to work every morning, focus on her Start-up Journey in the afternoon, get some exercise, and conserve money. Not only did she create a steady cash flow, she also rediscovered how great she felt when she biked and walked places, instead of jumping in her car every time she needed to go somewhere.

CAN I RUN A SUCCESSFUL BUSINESS AND STILL HAVE A LIFE?

If you are following the ideas and concepts put forth in this book, then of course the answer is yes! That's because you are realizing the value of connecting to your Inner Samurai and creating a business from the inside out. You know that you are one whole pie with many delicious pieces — not five, six, or eight separate pies.

All the pieces fit into one pie. Your work is one piece of the pie. Your family is another. Your friends, another. Other pieces include your physical and emotional well being, your wealth and financial health, and your service to your community.

You don't need to juggle anything. It can all flow beautifully together, one piece dovetailing nicely into another. This is called "having a life." This is lifestyle living — Inner Samurai style!

Can you run a successful business and still have a life? You bet! What does it take to do that? Listening to your inner voice, to your Inner Samurai. Your Inner Samurai is connected to all parts of you, all the time. It is connected to the Start-up Journey part of you while you are dining out with your friends. It is connected to the family part of you while you are working out. It is connected to your dreamtime while you are awake, connected to you, always, everywhere and anywhere.

Your Inner Samurai is the reason all the pieces of your pie taste great, both separately and together, and why one flavor doesn't overshadow the rest. Your Inner Samurai is the epitome of balance, zestful living, and expansive being. Your Inner Samurai is what contributes to your happiness of heart, to your wholeness of thinking, and to your richness of life.

Before Freda and I started working together, she thought she would have to stop everything she was doing and pour her whole self completely into starting up her business. Leslie had already put her family on notice that starting up a business meant she wasn't going to be able to spend as much time with them as she wanted. Kay had already resigned from two community boards she had enjoyed sitting on just because she thought she had to in order to make her start-up a success.

Does this sound like you? Do you think you have to give up having a life so you can start a business? Many of us do. Do you think you have to sacrifice your family, your friends, and the things you love to do, all for the sake of starting up your own business? Think again. Better yet, don't think. Listen. Go inward and listen to your Inner Samurai. Then you won't have to think. You will know.

Do I Have the Necessary Education and Experience To Do This?

I can point to three vital qualities that have contributed to the success of my clients: They have the courage to take the Start-up Journey, they have a vision, and they are guided by an inner-knowing that what they have to offer to the world matters.

As part of the Start-up Journey, one of the first things I do with my clients is create a vision statement. I can not emphasize enough how important creating a vision statement is for a small business start-up. It's darn important, folks! There's something about putting your vision down on paper that makes it real. Your vision is, after all, the whole reason for setting off on this journey in the first place. So take time to create your vision statement.

My client Chrissie's first vision statement looked like this after a couple of weeks of working on it together:

> Within the next three years, grow *Blue Heron* into a regional baby product delivery service providing food, nappies, and supplies to at-home mothers of newborns, infants and toddlers.

This statement beautifully focused on the vision she wanted to build for her business. Chrissie understood the Start-up Journey and the refinements and modifications that could occur. This statement left her enough wiggle room for growth and change, while aligning her with her purpose — to make it easy for women to be stay-at-home moms.

The second thing I address with my clients is the erroneous belief that they might not have the education or experience to start up a business. Most of the time my clients come in with a great deal of experience and education, but they don't realize its application to starting up a business. By focusing on what they have done in the past, we can quickly make a short list of what skills they might need to develop. They can work on acquiring these skills while they are starting up.

Just because you don't have a business degree doesn't mean you won't be successful at running a business. Accounting needs can be outsourced. Teleseminars can be taken. Books can be read. Questions can be asked. Experience can be gained. You don't have to do it all! Many of my clients are surprised to find out that I don't have a business degree. What I did have when I founded my first business, *Full Score Conducting*, and my second business, *Alkamae*, was a lot of experience running other people's businesses (both profit and not-for-profit), managing large groups of people and organizing huge projects.

I had what I like to call breadth-and-depth relevant experience. Through my professional church music ministry, counseling, university teaching, and conducting experience, I had created a storehouse and treasure-trove of applicable, relevant experience. You have one such treasure-trove, too. Whatever you don't have right now, you can learn.

WHAT IF I FAIL?

What if you don't? What if you don't fail? What then? It is better to have tried and lost than never to have tried at all — to embellish upon an oft-repeated phrase by Alfred Lord Tennyson.[4]

Letting the thought of failure come into your mind whenever you are embarking upon a new journey seems only natural. After all, none of us knows if we will fail or succeed at something new. We can, however, set the tone for success. And setting the tone makes all the difference.

Can you imagine Frodo setting off with the thought of not making it to Rivendell? Or those rushing across America during the California Gold Rush doing so with the thought of not finding gold? Or Much Afraid thinking she wouldn't make it to the High Places?

What about my client Rosemary? Can you imagine her considering her start-up a failure just because she ended up as a small business owner teaching other women how to make money flipping houses instead of becoming a relationship coach? Or would you call Helena a failure because she ended up as a freelance music critic instead of a piano tuner?

How about Chrissie? What would you think of her if I told you that during her Start-up Journey her transformation was so remarkable that she completely dropped her original vision statement and is now happily leading wine and food tours? She set herself up with a sweet business that runs specialty tours to Italy. She spends half the year touring around Italy with delightful food epicureans and wine tasters in tow, and the rest of the year dreaming up delicious spots to take her clients to next year.

Let yourself consider failure for as short a period of time as possible. Then move on. Repeat to yourself as many times a day as necessary:

Success is assured,

Greatness is,

Beauty surrounds, and

All is well.[5]

Success, greatness and beauty are your birthright. Remember what J. K. Rowling says in the opening quote of this chapter: "It is our choices . . . that show what we truly are, far more than our abilities."

NOTES FROM YOUR INNER SAMURAI

My will shall shape the future. Whether I fail or succeed shall be no man's doing but my own. I am the force; I can clear any obstacle before me or I can be lost in the maze. My choice; my responsibility; win or lose, only I hold the key to my destiny.

— Elaine Maxwell

- Cultivate the art of graciously accepting help. You never know who or what will come along to assist, guide or advise you.

- Consider reading *The Hero's Journey: The World of Joseph Campbell* or watch it on DVD.

- Get so familiar with The Heroine's Journey that you can pinpoint, in an instant, where you are along the journey, and spot it in others who are also beginning a journey of their own. It will save you a lot of gnashing of teeth and headaches.

- Search for feminine versions of The Hero's Journey in books, movies, and people. Read other women's autobiographies, take strength from their stories. Be inspired by their examples.

- Embrace the concept of lifestyle living, Inner Samurai style!

Redefine failure for yourself. As American magazine columnist, Marilyn vos Savant reminds us: "Being defeated is often a temporary condition. Giving up is what makes it permanent."

Chapter 7

THE STRENGTH OF INTUITION

For we walk by faith, not by sight.

— 2 Cor. 5:7

What is intuition? Have you ever really thought about that? The words *intuition*, *intuitive*, and *intuit* are all derived from the same Latin word *intueri* meaning "to see within." What, though, does intuition really mean? Webster's College Dictionary defines it as "direct perception of truth, fact, independent of any reasoning process; a keen and quick insight."[1] The Myers-Briggs Type Indicator, a personality questionnaire designed to identify certain psychological differences according to the typological theories of Carl Jung, explains that:

> Persons oriented toward intuition, process information by way of a 'sixth sense' or hunch... One who prefers the intuition function chooses to embrace the 'big picture.'[2]

How would you describe intuition? Some people I've talked to describe it as an instinctive knowing, an impression that something might be the case, a hunch, or a suspicion. Others describe it as an absolute knowing. Some think of it as a whole-istic way of knowing things, an integration of information. Still others talk about it as direct observation associated with the soul.

No matter how you describe intuition, we all have it. We are all intuitive. All of us, at one time or another, have had intuitive experiences — the kinds of experiences where we suddenly get an insight or information about something without clear reason. Sometimes we refer to it as a "gut feeling." Other times, it feels like a different kind of knowing.

One thing I've come to understand is that intuition is something quite different from the reasoning process of the mind. In fact, intuition seems to bypass the mind completely. It accesses direct knowledge without interference from rational thought. Here's how some well-known people talk about intuition:

- German-born American physicist Albert Einstein wrote, "The intuitive mind is a sacred gift and the rational mind is a faithful servant. We have created a society that honors the servant and has forgotten the gift."

- Swiss theologian Johann Kaspar Lavater talked about intuition as, "The clear conception of the whole at once."

- English poet, scholar, and novelist Robert Graves wrote, "Intuition is the supra-logic that cuts out all the routine processes of thought and leaps straight from the problem to the answer."

- Swedish-born American film and stage actress Ingrid Bergman said, "You must train your intuition — you must trust the small voice inside you which tells you exactly what to say, what to decide."

- American artist and metaphysical teacher Florence Scovel Shinn observed, "Intuition is a spiritual faculty and does not explain, but simply points the way."

- American physician and virologist Jonas Salk explained, "Intuition will tell the thinking mind where to look next."

I call intuition our Inner Samurai. "Inner," meaning within us all, and "Samurai," meaning strength. Together, our "Inner Samurai" points the way, guides us from within, and is the real deal.

WHAT INTUITION ISN'T

In order to understand intuition fully, it might be helpful to consider what it isn't. Intuition isn't common sense. Common sense relies on your personal philosophy or personal perspective about something, rather than a strong inner knower about the correct path to take or right decision to make. Intuition doesn't involve the process of reasoning.

Intuition is also not ESP, psychic ability, clairvoyance, or anything paranormal. There isn't someone or something outside of you channeling information or telling you what to do. Intuition is not a hunch, a suspicion, or a guess. Intuitive knowing is deeper and surer. Your intuition speaks clearly with a *yes* or *no* pulse from within.

Intuition isn't specifically a feeling or an emotion. True, right after the intuitive pulse, you may experience a wave of feeling or emotion, but this should not be mistaken for intuition itself. Here's the thing to keep in mind: First comes the *yes* or *no* pulse. It's that definitive. Then comes the wave of feeling or emotion. First the pulse, then the wave — that's the order.

Tapping into your Inner Samurai isn't difficult or complicated. All it takes is some practice.

I had been working with my client Lola for quite some time when one day she just blurted out, "Susan, you keep talking about getting connected to your Inner Samurai and feeling for her pulse, but I don't know how to do that!"

> "Ah," I replied, happy she let me know that she needed more information. "It's easy. You'll be able to do this in no time. Would you like to connect now?"
>
> "Yes. That would be great!"
>
> "Okay. Close your eyes and take a couple of deep breaths to calm and center yourself. Get in touch with your breath. Feel yourself relaxing."
>
> After a few moments I asked, "How are you doing with that?"
>
> "Great!"
>
> "Good. Now follow your breath inward, and sink into your body. Feel as if your eyes have sunken behind their eye sockets and you have removed yourself from the outer world to your inner world."

The Strength of Intuition

Ch. 7

Giving Lola 30 seconds to do that, I checked in. "Are you there?"

"Yes!" she beamed. "What a great feeling this is!"

"Yes, it is," I agreed. "Now all you need to do is ask your inner self — your Inner Samurai — a question. Yes or no questions work best. Also, ask questions that are stated for your highest good and greatest well-being, such as, 'Is it for my highest good and greatest well-being to go into partnership with Shelly?' Then wait for the pulse. Does that make sense?"

"Yes."

"Would you like to give it a go?"

"Yes."

"Okay. Think of any decision or issue facing you that you would like an inner answer to."

Lola thought for a moment. "I'd really like to know about a move I am contemplating to another state."

"Okay. Formulate the question to your highest good and greatest well-being."

"Is it in my highest good and greatest well being to move to New Mexico?" she asked. Then she paused.

"What pulse did you feel from your Inner Samurai? *Yes* or *no*?"

"No."

"Was there any chatter of explanation or rationalization after that pulse?" (I asked to make sure it was her Inner Samurai pulse she had experienced rather than the voice inside her head.)

121

"No, there wasn't."

"Okay. How do you feel about that answer?"

"Relieved, actually! As if space has opened up and I am sure and centered now."

That's how easy it is to tap into your Inner Samurai regarding any decision or issue facing you. And when you do, you will feel a pulse of *yes* or *no*. A pulse to move toward something or not. Your Inner Samurai never gives any long explanation or rationalization; that's your rational mind kicking in. Don't confuse your thinking mind with your intuitive knower. Don't mistake emotions and feelings for intuition.

Once you stop to think about it, it's easy to tell the difference between the rational mind kicking in with lots of chatter, explanation, and convincing, and the *yes*-or-*no* pulsing of your intuition. The minute you hear yourself explaining why something is a good idea or rationalizing why you shouldn't do something, you know you are in your head. It's pretty easy to catch yourself when your mind takes over. The tricky part comes when your feelings and emotions are involved.

FEELINGS AND EMOTIONS

Feelings and emotions sometimes coincide with the *yes* or *no* pulse from our Inner Samurai, and sometimes not. Let me explain. Feelings and emotions are generated as a response to something, either real or imagined. You can look at something and have a response. A beautiful sunset might evoke a feeling of warmth and happiness.

A horrific accident might create fear and dread. Those are waves of emotion running through you. The same could be said for all the rest of your five senses. Feelings and emotions can be evoked from something you hear, something you taste, something you smell, and something you touch.

The Inner Samurai pulse can also evoke a feeling. The most prevalent feeling that goes along with the *yes* pulse is a warm, glowing love that radiates outward. I have also experienced bubbling joy — the kind that feels like every cell in my body is dancing. Others have experienced what they call an inner smile or inner glow. I have yet to experience an Inner Samurai feeling that goes with the *no* pulse. It seems that our Inner Samurai attaches to a *yes* to propel us toward it, and this sometimes is accompanied by a feeling or emotion. The Inner Samurai simply doesn't attach, at all, to a *no*.

I've noticed another distinguishing characteristic of any feeling that accompanies the initial pulse of The Inner Samurai: It's "an inside job." This kind of emotion comes from within and radiates outward. After the pulse, it forms in the area of the heart. Then it opens up and radiates or bubbles outward from there, filling the body. Sometimes it feels like a flower opening; other times, like delicious soup warming the stomach on a cold day.

So, what about the *no*? Some people swear they have a negative feeling or emotion that accompanies their *no* pulse. My experience has been that the *no* that comes from our Inner Samurai is not attached to any negative feeling or emotion. It's just *no*. Interestingly, sometimes the emotion experienced with the *no* pulse is the same love and joy associated with the *yes* pulse.

So, if you think you are experiencing emotion around your *no* pulse, be careful. This emotion is most likely the voice inside your head — not your intuition — attaching itself to fear.

The Inner Samurai is direct and uncomplicated and doesn't chatter. So, if you tap into your Inner Samurai for some guidance and experience a simple *no* pulse, that is indeed your Inner Samurai speaking to you. If, on the other hand, you experience, "No! You shouldn't do that because it's really going to mess things up for you, and then you won't know what to do, and then you'll have to sort through everything," and on and on and on, that's just the voice inside your head.

WHAT CREATES OUR REALITY?

This is exactly the question my client Doris had when she contacted me about working on some *issues*, as she called them, getting her small business started. She informed me that once before she had almost been a business owner.

> "Almost been? What do you mean?" I asked, most intrigued.
>
> "Well, I was all but a small business owner."
>
> "All but? Almost? I have to hear this one. Tell me more."

Doris then shared a fascinating story that began fifteen years ago. She had been working for a large commercial real estate firm, managing one of their branch offices and doing very well for herself. She liked the hustle and bustle of activity around her and took pride in how she kept everyone organized and the office humming. At the time, Doris was 24. She had been out of school for a year when this office management position showed up, with promises of advancement. Commercial real estate was an interest of hers, so she decided she would take the job, learn all she could, and then open up a business of her own.

While at the real estate firm, Doris took an interest in John, one of the younger real estate agents, and soon they began dating. Over dinner, John would entertain her with stories of this client and that client and big properties he was working on. John also told her that he had dreams of making it big in commercial real estate and that he intended to strike out on his own some day.

As their relationship grew, John started asking Doris to stay late after work to help him with paperwork, which she was only too pleased to do. Soon, John was leaving her to do all the paper work while he went back out with clients to look at properties. His sales increased. Doris' knowledge increased. Doris discovered she liked filling out all the forms and checking to make sure everything was just right for John's clients. John liked having extra time to show more property.

Doris and John talked about getting married, opening up a business together, and living happily ever after. Instead of getting married, though, they moved in together to save money. Then they started up their commercial realty business.

This is where the "almost" part comes in. John had been able to spend extra time showing clients property because Doris had been doing his paperwork for him. Now he was the one with all the extra cash, not Doris. Of course, Doris hadn't minded that, then, because John had always said when they opened up a business together, they would be 50/50 partners.

As you are probably already predicting, that wasn't the case. John became the sole proprietor of their new business, rationalizing this to Doris. John continued going out and showing property to his new clients, and Doris managed the office and did all his paperwork. Whoops, I meant to say "their paperwork." They continued to talk about getting married, and even had a baby together. Now Doris was running the office, doing all the paperwork, and taking care of their child.

Doris was exhausted, irritable, and angry. One night she bundled up little Johnny and drove off in search of big Johnny. Three guesses where she found him. Nope, it wasn't with another woman. Nope, it wasn't with a client. It was at his other — unbeknownst to Doris — new office! He had just opened it with his old partner from the first commercial real estate place where he and Doris had met!

Doris was devastated. John didn't come home that night. Or the next night, or the next. He didn't show up at their office. He didn't return calls. Strangely, none of their clients ever called the office again, either. Doris checked their joint checking accounts. Yep, you guessed it. All the funds were gone. John, their money, and their clients had all vanished. Within a week, John's new business and business partner had disappeared as well.

Doris had been scammed, big time!

Five years later, Doris and Johnny Jr. were moving on from her shattered past with the help of family, friends, and support professionals. Surprisingly, Doris' dream of opening up a commercial real estate business was still intact. She was an expert at paperwork. She knew what went into managing an office. She had even gotten her real estate license and had been working in a real estate firm. She was smarter, she was wiser, she had money saved, and she was ready to get started when she came to see me.

Doris was very quick to grasp the Inner Samurai concept. It didn't take long for her to identify her Inner Samurai pulse, and to feel the difference between *yes* and *no*. She was having fun following her pulse and seeing the synchronistic events that popped up for her. She was enjoying how things were unfolding.

> One day she opened our coaching session with, "Susan, I really want to get this: What creates my reality?"
>
> "What we imagine creates our reality," I said, giving her plenty of room to maneuver.
>
> "Okay. My images create my reality." She tried this on for size. "These would be my thoughts?"
>
> "Yes."
>
> "So, what you are saying is that, literally, I can call into existence anything I want?"
>
> "Yes."
>
> "Like an act of creation."
>
> "Yes. The world that we live in is a world we have imagined, one we have thought of, one we have created, and it is the activity of imagining or thinking that has made it so."

"Is there anything you know of that is not produced by thought?"

"No."

"Oh, I see," she said. "So, I am the creator of my thoughts. That means what I make I can also unmake!"

"Yes! It also means that what you continue to think about sustains your reality."

Success, Inner Samurai Style

"So, what gets in our way, Susan? What keeps us from being successful, from moving forward, towards the things we want?"

"You mean besides professional scam artists," I teased her.

"Yes," she laughed.

Together, Doris and I explored the many thought patterns that could be getting in the way of her success. In the end, she narrowed them down to:

- Her beliefs
- Her thoughts about the past
- Her unwillingness to accept full responsibility

Beliefs Are Repeated Thoughts That Have Hardened Into Facts

For the longest time, people believed that the world was flat. Twenty-five hundred years ago, the

The Strength of Intuition

Ch. 7

Greeks came along and theorized that the Earth was round. Despite this, most people continued to sustain the belief that the world was flat. When Ferdinand Magellan and the crew of the Victoria confirmed that the world was round by circling the globe on a three-year voyage from 1519-1522, maps had to be redrawn, geography books rewritten, and new thoughts accepted.

This is a powerful example of what happens when a repeated thought turns into a belief that hardens into a fact. Nothing else can be thought. No other thought can be considered outside the sustained belief.

Doris believed that she and John would be married, open a business together, and live happily ever after. She sustained that belief, despite mounting evidence to the contrary.

Doris doesn't stand alone. We all have clung to outdated or unrealistic beliefs. Do you recall a time when you stood on "facts" despite the evidence? You believed what you wanted to believe, didn't you? You believed what you kept telling yourself despite what you were seeing with your own eyes or feeling from the inside. It happens all the time — to individuals, groups, and even entire nations.

Looking back, Doris laughed when she recalled some of the things she told herself about John, their relationship, their business, and their life. "I used to tell people I didn't mind doing all John's paperwork for him. After all, he was working so hard for us." We laughed at that for a moment before she recalled something else. "When I got pregnant, I really put a lot of pressure on John to get married. I wanted us to be a family. But John kept putting me off. So, I just kept telling myself that once the business settled down, we'd get married." Doris held onto that belief even after she discovered John had opened another business and wiped out all their bank accounts. She kept saying to herself, "There must be some mistake; John wouldn't do this to us."

Beliefs are powerful. Hardened into fact, they become blinding, limiting, and self-defeating. Hardened facts cage us in and cut us off from our Inner Samurai and intuitive knowing. They enclose us and stop our growth. To grow we must be open to new thoughts and new ideas. We must be open to our Inner Samurai.

Next time you find yourself crossways with a "truth" or "fact," consider that your truth may need to be explored, revisited, and revised. Make it a habit to check in with your Inner Samurai. Ask, "Is there something that would be in my higher good and greater well being to view differently?" Then, listen to what she says.

THE PAST IS PAST

Whether it's a break-up, a tragic accident, or a scam such as Doris experienced, it's hard not to stop asking "Why?" Doris said she asked this question repeatedly: "Why did this happen to me?" She just couldn't get her mind around how she had been so gullible, so blind, so trusting. Why didn't she see the clues that were there? For a long time, she said she felt angry with John; then, even angrier with herself. She searched for two years to find him to try and recover the stolen money. And always there were the questions: "Why? Why did this happen? Why did he do this to me?"

After exhausting her friends, family, and herself with her continued replaying of the past, she turned to a professional therapist for help. Together, they began the healing journey — out of the past and into the present. What Doris learned along the way was that the past is in the past. By continuing to revisit it, she was actually re-activating *that* energy in the present. This was causing her to loop into herself in an ever-continuing circle of pain, anger, doubt, and confusion.

She also learned that her images of the past, stored in her memory, were faulty and one-sided. That's how it is for all of us. Memories are one-sided, seen from one perspective — ours. Those memories can never be expected to produce answers to the question, "Why?"

Doris eventually concluded that she either could continue to revisit and re-enact her past, or she could begin to build her future by focusing on her present. The minute she made the decision to "step into the light," as she put it, she felt a shift inside. Deep down inside. It was if something came alive. That coming alive was her Inner Samurai, her *yes*.

The minute Doris focused her attention, her Inner Samurai was connected, engaged, and activated. That's because our Inner Samurai's point of power is only in the present. Doris remembers the moment it happened: "I had been thinking about John and what had gone wrong for the umpteenth time. I was feeling miserable, alone, and angry. I was mad at John, mad at myself, and angry with God for letting this happen. Then, little Johnny walked solemnly into the room, put his little hands on my arms, looked me straight in the eye, and said 'Mommy happy. Mommy happy — now.'"

At that moment, Doris said she felt something click within. Immediately, her heart burst open, she began to cry. She hugged little Johnny fiercely to her. As he struggled to get free, they both tumbled to the floor. Doris started tickling him. Amidst his shrieks of joy, she looked at her precious son and said "Mommy's happy now. Let's go build a happy life together!"

Next time you find yourself revisiting the past and asking all those "why?" questions, consider that you might be happier focusing on your present. Check in with your Inner Samurai. Ask, "Would it be in my highest good and greatest well being to focus on my present?" Then wait for the pulse.

It's All about You

Author and marketing guru Joe Vitale says, "The hardest concept for most people to grasp is that they are the sole reason they are experiencing whatever they have in their lives. They are totally responsible."[3] And he's right. Accepting full responsibility for your life takes guts. It takes courage. It takes willingness to own it all — the good, the bad, the wonderful. It's also the best way to strengthen both your relationship with your Inner Samurai and your intuition.

> "How do I do that?" Doris asked one day. "How do I strengthen my intuition?"
>
> "First thing to do is pay attention to it. Get really good at listening for that pulse."
>
> "Okay, I can do that."

> "The next thing to do is to decide what you want. So, let's focus on your new real estate business. Do you want to own a branch office, or do you want to start a specialty real estate business?"
>
> "I want to start my own business, and I want to cater to single moms and dads who want to provide a home for their children."

Doris wanted to take all she had learned from her traumatic experience and help other single moms and dads stabilize their home life as easily as possible. She named her business *Happy Homes Real Estate* and immediately took on a partner. She didn't have any qualms about doing so, despite what happened to her in the past. That's because she collaborated with the best partner in the world — her Inner Samurai.

Next, Doris and I began the work of envisioning the perfect location for her business, her ideal clients, the hours she wanted to work, and how much money she wanted to bring in.

> "How do I do all that in the shortest amount of time?" Doris wanted to know one day.
>
> "The key is to commit yourself to the *feeling* of your wish fulfilled. Live as if what you want has already come to pass. Start first with imagining happy moms, dads, and children in their brand new homes. Feel what a great experience they had with you as their realtor. Feel them shaking hands with you as you turn over their keys to them. Look into their eyes and see the joy and happiness in their smiles. Hear the words of thanks they say to you, and smell their cologne or perfume as they hug you in gratitude. See them giving your business

card to friends of theirs. Hear them singing your praises. Feel the lightness in your step as you walk away. See yourself depositing your check and feeling wonderful about the amount of money you earned. See and hear your family and friends cheering for you. As New Thought teacher Goddard Neville says: 'Enter the image of the wish fulfilled, then give it sensory vividness and tones of reality by mentally acting as you would act were it a physical act.'"[4]

"That sounds like fun!" she giggled.

"It is! Imagining the wish fulfilled always brings about a union with that state. However, the key to all this is to embody the image. Live in it. Function in it. Think from within it, rather than thinking *of* or *upon it*."

"Hmm ...," Doris pondered, "That sounds like a subtle difference."

"That's what it may seem like to you now. Once you start thinking, being, and acting *from within it* you will notice the big difference between *from within* and *thinking of*. It's the difference between looking at a picture and looking out from a picture. The difference between looking at the building you want to own from the outside and actually being inside the building, answering phones, and looking up from your desk as your happy clients come through the door."

"Okay. And this is the shortest way to manifest what I want?"

"Yes."

"Is there anything I can do to mess this up?"

"Yes. You can try to make things happen, rather than allowing your Inner Samurai to unfold things naturally for you. You can ignore your intuition and start taking effortful action. You can keep changing your mind. You can believe what so-called *reality* is showing you. By constantly comparing what you are imagining with what *reality* is showing, you will hold what you want away from you, in some distant place and time in the future."

"Wow! So what you are saying is that, as long as I go about my day as if what I want is already here, it will happen?"

"Yes. Capture the feeling. Live in the feeling. Enjoy everything about your new business, now."

A couple of weeks later, Doris checked in. As expected, some things had begun to manifest for her. She was getting calls at her home office from single moms and dads wanting to purchase homes. She even had her first referral. Even though she had not yet brought into her outer world the inner vision she had been imagining about her perfect business location, she could feel it coming to her. "It's no longer a matter of *if*," she proclaimed, "It's only a matter of *when*."

A month after that, Doris had sold her first home under her new business name. Her clients were so happy, they sent her flowers as a thank you. Doris added the sight and smell of flowers on her desk to her acting *from within it* imagining process.

Three months after she began acting as if she was already in her dream location, Doris actually moved into her dream location, physically. That afternoon, she and little Johnny went out to dinner to celebrate.

On their way home, Doris stopped to show Johnny where her new business was. As she was wandering around and Johnny was crawling beneath desks, there was a knock at the door. Startled, they both looked up to see a woman standing there with a bouquet of flowers in her hand. The woman said "Hi, I'm your next door business neighbor. These flowers were left for you earlier today." Doris thanked her for the flowers, and then opened the card and read: "Congratulations on your new office space. We wish you lots of success and happiness. Love, Mom and Dad." Here were the flowers she'd envisioned on the desk in her new space.

> Doris paused in the telling of the story. When she spoke again, she said, "It really is all about me, isn't it?"
>
> "Yes."
>
> "Me and my Inner Samurai."
>
> "Yes!"
>
> "I can live from within that."

We talked some more and then signed off in the rosy glow of Doris' success. I'm happy to report that, at the time of this writing, Doris has been in business for two years now. Johnny is eight years old and continues to be a fountain of inspiration and joy. Doris thinks very little about John or what happened in the past. She is happy and at peace with herself and her world.

Next time you find yourself wanting circumstances or situations to change, consider creating change as quickly as possible through the power of acting *from within*. Check in with your

Inner Samurai. Ask, "Is imagining my wish already fulfilled in my highest good and greatest well-being the best way to go?" Then wait for the pulse.

NOTES FROM YOUR INNER SAMURAI

For whereas the mind works in possibilities, the intuition works in actualities, and what you intuitively desire, that is possible to you. Whereas what you mentally or 'consciously' desire is nine times out of ten impossible; hitch your wagon to a star, or you will just stay where you are.

— D. H. Lawrence

- Practice listening to your Inner Samurai's *yes* or *no* pulse. Become good at distinguishing it from the chatter of the voice inside your head.

- When in doubt about your feelings and emotions, feel for the pulse. Your Inner Samurai pulse is right 100% of the time.

- Remember that your mind can operate out of fear. Don't let fear stand in your way. Go into the fear to release its hold on you.

- Know the power of your thoughts. Choose the good ones.

- Be wary of belief systems, facts, and truths. Question your truths daily.

- Spend as little time on the "whys" of the past as possible. Focus, instead, on the "whats" of your present. Build for the future.

- It is all about you. Always.

Part III

Discovering Your Inner Samurai

Chapter 8

WHAT IN THE HECK IS RESISTANCE?

EFFORTLESS ACTION AND THE INNER SAMURAI

To make a dream come true, one must have a dream, believe in it, and work toward it. Often it is essential that another significant person believe that the dream is possible: that person is a vision carrier whose faith is often crucial.

— Jean Shinoda Bolen

What resistance is or is not certainly has many people confused. Becoming a successful small business owner, a solopreneur, or entrepreneurial woman requires you to know the answer.

Women in particular seem to become more hung up in the vibrational energy of resistance than men. Although I'm not sure why that is, I do have a couple of ideas. Perhaps it is because men have been acculturated to disregard their intuitive, internal knowing in favor of a more direct approach to things. This could be one reason why they seem able to push through their resistance more readily than women do. Another reason might have to do with how society has encouraged men to develop and rely upon the left side of their brain hemisphere when making decisions. Regardless of the reason, men do seem to be able to push through their resistance more easily than women, which may or may not be a good thing.

In general, women are more sensitive to rejection than men are. Let's say that two small business owners — one male and one female — were feeling the same degree of resistance to moving forward with their businesses. The man most likely would try to figure out what was going on by taking a hard look at his business. The woman would turn inward and look at herself. The man would look at his business with a critical eye toward what is going wrong. The woman would turn her critical eye toward herself. This fundamental difference and approach to resistance makes this chapter a very important one for anyone experiencing resistance in their business, especially women.

THE MANY FACES OF RESISTANCE

As a small business coach and consultant, I hear many stories from many women. Stories about why something isn't working and questions about what is going wrong. These women think their stories are about business. More often than not, these stories have less to do with business and more to do with resistance.

What in the Heck is Resistance?
Effortless Action and the Inner Samurai

Ch. 8

The other day, I was flying back from a conference I attended in Denver. I struck up a conversation with the woman sitting next to me, whose name was Sophie. In due course, we got around to asking each other, "So, what do you do for a living?" I told her I was a small business coach and consultant for entrepreneurial women wanting to transform their lives and make a difference in the world by starting up their own specialty business.

> "Wow!" Sophie seemed intrigued. "How do you do that?"
>
> "By taking the fear out of starting up," I said.
>
> "Boy, I sure could have used you when I was starting up my business," she said, shaking her head in dismay. "I bet you could have saved me a lot of frustration, heartache, and pain."
>
> "What happened?" I asked, settling into my seat, getting ready to hear her story.
>
> "Well..." she began, and two hours later finished with, "It was the most personally devastating experience of my life."

In between, Sophie told me that her long-held, deeply cherished dream was to own a gourmet chocolate business. She had a handful of secret family recipes for making unique and delicious chocolate desserts, handed down to her through five generations of women. Her mother's side of the family had come from Austria, and her great-great grandmother, Jocilla, had been a well respected chocolatier in Salzburg.

Sophie came with her parents to America when she was a young child. Both parents were working hard to provide for the family, and Sophie was often left alone. Her mom didn't have much time for anything more than getting their regular family meals on the table, so Sophie asked her mom if she could help out by making desserts. Her mother, glad to be relieved of the burden of making time-consuming desserts, gladly turned that responsibility over to her young daughter. Sophie couldn't have been more pleased.

One day when she was ten, Sophie asked if she could bake a cake for her father's upcoming birthday. Using Great-Great Grandmother Jocilla's famous sacher torte recipe, Sophie's passion for chocolate was launched. First, she made the nearly flourless cake with butter, eggs, bittersweet chocolate and sugar. Next was the dark rum and apricot filling. Finally, she created the bittersweet glaze. All the while, Sophie's focus and attention to detail were fierce. A chocolate aficionado was born!

Thirty years later, with her own two children nearly grown and out of the house, Sophie returned to her dream of becoming a chocolatier. With the support of her husband and the enthusiastic backing of her teenaged sons, who had long enjoyed her creations, she got started. Long on knowing everything about chocolate and short on knowing anything about starting up a business, Sophie relied heavily on the advice and help of friends, family, and relatives. To her credit, she took a couple of business classes at her local community college, read all she could about starting up a small business, enrolled in an online marketing class, and had the expertise of one-time business owner Uncle Maximilian to guide her.

This story has a sad ending, as you may already have surmised. Sophie's dream never got off the ground. After pouring a tremendous amount of time, energy, and money into the venture, she became overwhelmed with all the work of running a business. She was confused about what to do first or next and frustrated with everyone's well-meaning advice. Her dream buried under a pile of bills, Sophie went into a period of deep depression. She stopped making chocolate altogether, even for her own family. Everywhere she went, she was met with well-meaning consolers. "Ah, too bad," they all said. "It was such a great idea."

That was five years ago. Sophie's children are both in college now. Today she spends her time keeping busy, working here and there cleaning houses, taking in sewing, and occasionally baking cakes for special occasions. "I'm lost," she confided. "I'm lost without my dream."

> "What happened?" I gently asked. "What do you think went wrong?"
>
> "I didn't know what I was doing," she sighed. "I didn't know how to get my product out there. I just assumed people would line up to buy my chocolates. I didn't know how much work it was to start up a business. I was afraid I would never be able to make it work."
>
> "That happens to a lot of people," I assured her. "Especially women."
>
> "Oh?"

"Yes. You would not believe the number of my clients who have said the very same things. It's impossible to know how much work it really does take to start up a business unless you've done it before. Every one of us who has ever started up a business has been afraid that it would fail."

"Really? I had no idea," she said, relief mixed with regret in her voice.

Do you see yourself in Sophie's story? If so, take comfort. This is a common scenario for many would-be small business owners. Sadly, throwing in the towel is the most frequent response. What happened? What went wrong? Once you were bright-eyed with excitement. Now, you're doubled over with doubt, confusion, and hurt.

"Maybe this wasn't such a good idea," you begin.

"I guess it just wasn't meant to be," you conclude.

What's Really Going On?

Hold the phone! More to the point, hold the baby and don't throw her out with the bath water! Before you chuck that great idea, give up your dream, or settle for something else, you owe it to yourself to find out what's really going on. Knowing how to start up a business is only half the equation of a successful small business start-up. The other half is knowing how to deal with all the anxiety, frustration, confusion, and overwhelm, along with the fear of even starting a business. In short, you need to know how to recognize and cope with resistance.

What in the Heck is Resistance?
Effortless Action and the Inner Samurai

Ch. 8

Every new business starts out with great passion, fun, and excitement. Then things become harder and less fun. This is because you have encountered resistance, usually in the form of doubt, frustration, and confusion. This is normal. Everyone hits the wall of resistance. In fact, most of us hit it many times when starting up a business. Let me say this again. It's normal. When you are living high on the excitement of your dream, your allowance is high and your resistance low. With this mindset, success is assured and action is effortless.

It isn't until later, after the newness has worn off, that things just naturally become harder and less fun. During this period, getting your business up and running is fraught with details and the need to make seemingly endless decisions. This is when your resistance starts overtaking your allowance. Eventually, the entire process spirals downward until you hit bottom. By then, your resistance is very high and your allowance is very low. This is when Sophie threw in the towel.

Is this sounding familiar? Perhaps you, too, have thrown in your towel.

TIMING IS EVERYTHING

When is it the right time to throw in the towel? How do you know if it's time to cut your losses or regroup and move forward? How do you know if you have hit the wall of resistance or an actual dead-end? The worst time to answer these questions is when you are at the height of your frustration, doubt, and despair. That is definitely the worst possible time for you to think about throwing in the towel!

What you need to do instead is recognize your resistance for what it is and come out the other side. You need to recognize what resistance is actually saying to you. The more quickly you do this, the better.

Resistance carries with it a vibration of opposition. Opposition to what? To change. There is a prevailing belief in the West that says creating or manifesting anything takes struggle. Sophie was taught that following her dream of becoming a world-class chocolatier had to take great effort, striving, and sacrifice. Of course, that's true. Achieving excellence does take a lot of time and energy, single-minded devotion, and focused effort. Working on a dream-come-true can be risky. But, and here's the important part: *It doesn't have to be a struggle.* Let me say it again. Manifesting your dream doesn't have to be the struggle that everyone assumes it has to be.

EFFORTLESS ACTION TO THE RESCUE

How is this possible? By learning to adopt something called "effortless action." Once you tap into your Inner Samurai, effortless action will become available to you.

Effortless action is Inner Samurai action. It is inspired action. It is action flowing outward from within, rather than outward action taken without any inner connection. Effortlessness is the *Inner* part of Inner Samurai. Action is the *Samurai* part of Inner

Samurai. Together, they form the quintessential partnership of a successful small business start-up.

Inspired action is action motivated by joy, excitement, and eagerness. You know you are taking effortless, inspired action when you can't wait to jump out of bed in the morning. When you can't wait to see what's going to happen next. Effortless action is timeless action. The old adage, "time flies when you're having fun," takes on new meaning. In a state of effortless action, time will fly. You will be "in the zone" (as my computer programmer friends like to say when they are working on code). You'll have energy to burn. Doesn't that sound great?

So, what's the problem?

In the West, we place great value on struggling hard for the things we want. We reward those who work hard and struggle. We bow down before and heap respect upon people who have made a name for themselves through toil and labor. We have a high opinion of those who have conquered their fears, overcome hardships, and pulled themselves up by their bootstraps. Perhaps you have heard your parents saying, "You've got to work hard to get someplace in this world."

Our society validates and rewards those who paddle upstream against a strong current. In the West, we have made struggle synonymous with success. However, what is really being rewarded isn't the person who succeeds — it's the struggle itself. It's the action of pushing past resistance and fear.

I wonder . . . has this been good for us? Is it a good thing that we have raised generations of people to ignore their emotions, deny their inner guidance system, and suppress their Inner Samurai? I don't think so. Maybe after reading this book, you won't think so, either.

WHAT IS RESISTANCE?

Resistance is based upon the assumption that there needs to be a struggle in order to effect or create change. That's just plain hogwash. When you are tuned into your Inner Samurai and following her direction, there is no need to struggle. When you do tune in, you will hear her wise counsel: *Don't struggle to change the experience, allow the experience to change on its own.* When you allow the experience to change, rather than try to manage, manipulate, or control it, you have released your hold on any intended outcome. Now you stand in a place of equanimity, complete with calm and composed power. You are standing at the center of your Inner Samurai. From here, resistance is immediately released. Action becomes effortless. Action becomes inspired.

Resistance is an attempt to control reality. Controlling reality is not the same as having self-control. Controlling reality is your ego at work. Self-control is your Inner Samurai's strength and equanimity. It's a balanced, levelheaded, poised state that neither grasps for something nor has an aversion to anything. In this state, you do not praise or place blame. You do not identify with success or failure. You do not stress over right or wrong action. You open to inspired action. Instead of being limited by resistance, you allow and become limitless.

Allow what? Anything. Allow anything to occur. Allow the possibility of all things. This is powerful medicine, as my Native American friends say.

Resistance, on the other hand, holds you away from what you want. What would happen if you stopped paddling upstream? If you turned and went with the current? That may be a pretty scary thought. You've been struggling against the current for so long that putting your paddles inside the boat and letting the current take you feels downright unnatural. Yet, that is exactly what the messenger of resistance is telling you to do. Imagine what it would feel like simply to *allow* whatever changes you want to occur, to occur. All of us are in a constant state of change and transformation, all the time. Our Inner Samurai knows this. Our Inner Samurai allows for this.

Resistance is the number one thing that will stop you in your tracks. That is what stopped Sophie. How many times has resistance stopped you?

Fear Is Not Resistance

Don't confuse fear — real fear — with resistance. When you experience fear, you act out of the vibration of powerlessness. Fear jettisons you into fight-or-flight mode.

By contrast, when you experience resistance, you stay put and try to figure things out. You become fixated on the problem and keep asking that dead-end question: "Why?" Unlike resistance, fear doesn't think, fixate, or question. Fear acts.

Energetically, the powerlessness of fear feels quite different from the opposition of resistance. Test it out.

Think this thought: Fear. How did your body respond to the thought of fear? Did you notice your eyes dilating? Did you experience rapid and shallow breathing? Did your eyes narrow and dart around the room looking for an escape route or assault weapon? Could you feel your body winding-up, getting ready to spring? The image that always comes to my mind is the scene in a movie when a barn is on fire, and frightened horses are trapped inside. The minute someone comes to the stalls to release them, the horses bolt, eyes wide, nostrils flaring, hooves pounding the ground as they barrel out of the barn.

Now, think this thought: Opposition. How did your body respond to that thought? Did you feel your arms crossing protectively in front of your chest? Did you notice your feet spreading apart, taking a wider stance? Could you feel your breath deepening in preparation for a standoff? Think Wyatt Earp at the O.K. Corral. Remember in the movie version how the Earp brothers and Doc Holliday looked while striding down Fremont Street, in Tombstone, Arizona? Their bodies were tense, their faces taut, and their stance purposeful right before they drew on the Clanton brothers and Tom McLaury? That's opposition.

Fear expresses itself in short, one-word phrases. Run! Go! The voice of powerlessness and fear sounds like a command. That's because the part of the brain that functions when you are in fear is the reptilian brain, the brain stem. The reptilian brain acts on stimulus and response. It makes quick decisions without thinking. The reptilian brain is driven by fear, focuses on survival, and takes over when you feel threatened or endangered.

What in the Heck is Resistance?
Effortless Action and the Inner Samurai

Ch. 8

The voice of opposition and resistance often sounds like a question. What is holding me back? What am I afraid of? It can also sound like a statement. "Over my dead body!" And the Dirty Harry mantra, "Go ahead — make my day." Resistance expresses itself in complete sentences. That's because the neocortex part of the brain governs your ability to speak, think, and solve problems. It is the most evolutionary, advanced part of your brain and affects your creativity and ability to learn.

Think back to Sophie's story. Was it time for her to throw in the towel, or was she just facing the wall of resistance? Did she confuse her frustration and fear of failure with actual fear? Was her flight based on actual reptilian brain-based fear? No. It was a result of her thinking mind's response to a high degree of resistance. Sophie threw in the towel too soon.

OUR BUDDIES, THE REPTILIAN BRAIN AND NEOCORTEX

Governed by the reptilian brain, fear bypasses the neocortex and mobilizes the body into action. Whether real or imagined, fear is a powerful biological reaction that kicks in when you feel threatened physically. Fear prepares you for fight or flight. To attack or run. Fear is a strategic weapon that only operates in survival mode. If you are in survival mode, you won't need to ask yourself the question, "What am I afraid of?" You will know.

On a no-fear-to-great-fear scale of one to ten, fear is a ten. Feeling afraid is a seven or eight. Feeling terrified is an eight or nine. When you are feeling afraid or terrified, you can still think. You are still operating out of your neocortex. Once you hit ten, though, you're cooked. You've dropped down into your brain stem and are galvanized to action.

Resistance is your neocortex alarm bell alerting you to opposition. On the scale of no-resistance-to-great resistance, slight uneasiness is a one. Four or five is confusion. Upward from that are agitation, frustration, inertia, and anger. Worry, guilt, and self-doubt weigh in at the three or four mark. Discouragement and scarcity range between three and nine, depending on the intensity of the feeling.

The higher you go up the scale of resistance, the more opposition you feel. The more opposition you feel, the more immobilized you become. Your degree of immobilization is directly proportional to how important something is to you. Pushing through or ignoring your resistance makes things worse. To make things better, discover the answer to the question, *What do I need to allow?*

Imagine what it would have been like if Sophie had asked herself that question. *What do I need to*

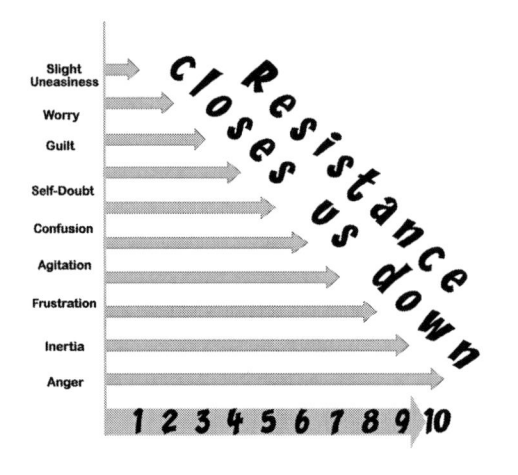

allow? That one question would have made all the difference in the world to her. That one question would have helped her soften her resistance. It would have given her some perspective, some relief. Why? Because the vibration of allowance is the opposite of the vibration of resistance. Allowance holds no opposition. It lies at the opposite end of the continuum. Resistance closes us down. Allowance opens us up.

Hope Floats in the Direction of Your Greatest Allowing

When Sophie hit her wall of resistance, do you think she was feeling open and expansive or closed and contracted? When she decided to throw away her dream of becoming a chocolatier and business owner, do you think she wanted to give up? Do you think she thought she had any other option? Probably not. Based on her vantage point, her nose pressed flat against the wall of resistance, Sophie made the only decision she knew how to make. She traded her dream for depression.

Sophie is not unique. Her story is but one among many that I have heard through the years. It happens in business relationships and personal relationships. It happens with financial matters and career choices.

However, there is hope. Hope floats on Sir Isaac Newton's Third Law of Motion: "For every action, there is an equal and opposite reaction." Vibrationally, allowance is the opposite response to resistance. Allowance is the key to figuring out what's really going on with you. What's behind your resistance? Figure out that piece of the puzzle, and you will know what's been slowing you down, holding you back, and making you want to throw in the towel.

Turn resistance on its ear. Next time you hit the wall of resistance, turn immediately in the equal and opposite direction — away from resistance and toward allowance. Ask, *What do I need to allow?* Then stand back and let the magic happen. By asking that one simple yet powerful question, you have entered the domain of your Inner Samurai. That one question will cause your Inner Samurai to light up.

Turn away from the wall of resistance. Turn in the direction of allowance — in the direction of your Inner Samurai. Ask the question. Allow hope to float. If Sophie had done that, you might be enjoying one of her gourmet chocolates right now, and she might be enjoying the rewards of a successful small business.

NOTES FROM YOUR INNER SAMURAI

> *The more you see yourself as what you'd like to become, and act as if what you want is already there, the more you'll activate those dormant forces that will collaborate to transform your dream into your reality.*
>
> — Wayne Dyer

- Hold onto the baby while you are throwing out the bath water. Throwing them both out together will cause great heartache and loss.

- Recognize resistance for what it is. All resistance is resistance to change. Changing from the known to the unknown. The unknown is nothing to fear. It's just the unknown. Everyone experiences resistance to change. It's normal. Get over it.

- Get familiar with the many faces of resistance. Guilt, confusion, anger, frustration, terror, doubt, and scarcity are just a few.

- Acknowledge that fear is not resistance. There are very few things that actually compel us into fight-or-flight mode. That's good news! The rest is just resistance, and you know how to handle that.

- Get in touch with your Inner Samurai by asking that all-important question, "What do I need to allow?" By doing so, you will move inward to your greatest source of strength and knowing.

- Never force outcome. Form a partnership with your Inner Samurai and summon effortless and inspired action from within.

- Above all else, remember that manifesting your dream doesn't have to be the struggle you've heard it's supposed to be. It can be joy. Let it be joy.

Chapter 9

THE ART OF GOAL SETTING

There's nothing wrong with goals and trying to fulfill them — as long as the main focal point of your attention remains the present moment. It's like being on a journey and knowing where you want to get to, but realizing at the same time that the entire journey ultimately consists of one step — the step you're taking at this moment. That one step is all there ever is, and so you give it your fullest attention. In other words, the step you're taking now is primary, the destination — the goal — is secondary. If the destination becomes primary, you will become stressed and anxious and you will miss life. You will suffer, and the destination will not make you happy even when you get there, when you attain your goals.

— Eckhart Tolle

The problem with goals is that they are made in the present, to be fulfilled in the future. But the present is always changing. That means the future is always changing, too. So, if you've created a static goal for a future time in a dynamic and ever changing present, it's almost impossible to attain that goal. This is why, after the first couple of weeks of working toward your goal, setbacks occur, and before you know it, you're off the mark. You're struggling to get back on task, wondering if you will ever reach your goal. If only you had known about the 60-40 Inner Samurai Rule.

What is the 60-40 Inner Samurai Rule? This rule states that, once you set a goal, 60% of your action is to be taken in the now. Only 40% of your action is to be taken in the future. This rule takes into account the dynamic, ever changing present that we all live in. It also sets the intention for your goal to be fulfilled. That's because being in this 60-40 zone puts you in energetic vibration with prosperity and abundance. Manifestation then becomes just a matter of time. That's it. Chapter over. Bye Bye!

Of course, you can increase the percentage of action to be taken in the present to 70%, 80%, even 90% or more. The higher the percentage of action in the now, the faster manifestation will occur. Of course, there still has to be some percentage in the future — after all, that's what makes it a goal — even if it's just 2%. Still, anything less than 60% in the now is just a wish, a want, a dream that may never be fulfilled. Don't waste your time setting goals if you aren't committed to spending 60% of your action toward your goal right now.

The Deliciousness of Wanting More

Sarah is a classic example of the kind of entrepreneurial woman who comes to me for coaching. She is bright, articulate, and classy. She is excited about life, creative in her vision, and confident in her direction. She is ready to start up a business. She comes to our coaching calls sparked with enthusiasm, anticipation, and a willingness to perform. Sarah is a player. (No, not a player in *that* definition of the word.) She's a player because she is ready to *bring it*, ready to get involved. Like most of my clients, Sarah doesn't waste time. And, like most of my clients, Sarah invites fresh perspectives and is raring to go.

By most standards, Sarah is already a success. She has a good life. She lives well, has a nice home, loving family, and great friends. She travels, shops, and spends money as she wishes. She volunteers her time and contributes to organizations that are meaningful and important to her. Sarah knows herself well and has done a lot to improve herself. But . . . she wants more. More of the things she loves.

She wants more money, more time, more travel, and relationships that are more loving. She comes to our coaching calls ready to be nudged out of her comfort zone into a new way of thinking, being, and having. She insists on me being forthright and direct in my communication. She wants more from our sessions than handholding. She wants more than a feel-good experience. She wants something measurable that she can walk away with and apply immediately. As I've said, Sarah wants more.

PHYSICAL NEED OR EMOTIONAL NEED?

Wanting more can be a great feeling. It can also be like torture. Seems to me there are really two sides to wanting more. There is the side that comes from incompleteness and the side that comes from completeness. One holds the energetic vibration of lack and scarcity, the other holds the energetic vibration of prosperity and abundance.

Confused? Many people are. That's because most of us use the word "need" when we really mean "want."

"I need you to get up right now and get ready for school," a frustrated mom might say to her eight-year-old so she doesn't have to drive him to school if he misses the bus.

"I need a drink," your co-worker might say after a particularly hard day at work.

"I need you to pick me up a Starbucks double latte on your way back from lunch," an executive might say to her administrative assistant.

None of these things are needs. They are wants. They are wants stated as needs for emotional emphasis.

"I need to stabilize my electrolytes," a long distance runner might say after running the Boston Marathon.

"You need to pay that electric bill so we don't freeze to death," a stay-at-home mother might say to her partner after receiving the second shut-off notice.

"I need air," an asthma sufferer might choke out when trying to grasp a breath.

These are examples of real needs. Real physical needs. The kind of needs that are critical to life support.

In 1943, psychologist Abraham Maslow wrote a paper entitled *A Theory of Human Motivation*. In it, he presented his now famous "Hierarchy of Needs" that outlined the continuum of needs that runs from actual physiological to self-actualized needs. The pyramid is read from bottom to top. The basic, physical needs for survival, such as air, food, water, shelter, and security are at the base. Next come safety, love, and self-esteem, with self-actualization at the top.

Maslow's theory contends that it is only when our basic physical needs are met can we move on to satisfying our higher emotional wants. The lowest tier of the pyramid holds the energetic vibration of lack and scarcity. When you are struggling just to put food on the table, have clean water to drink, or are fighting to take a breath of air, you are in physical need. Critical survival need. Things at this level are dire, and sustaining life is all that's important.

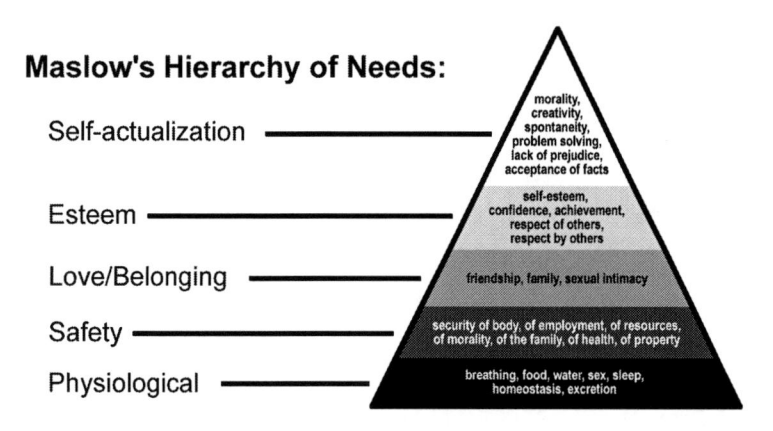

Maslow's Hierarchy of Needs:

Self-actualization — morality, creativity, spontaneity, problem solving, lack of prejudice, acceptance of facts

Esteem — self-esteem, confidence, achievement, respect of others, respect by others

Love/Belonging — friendship, family, sexual intimacy

Safety — security of body, of employment, of resources, of morality, of the family, of health, of property

Physiological — breathing, food, water, sex, sleep, homeostasis, excretion

Once your physiological needs are met and you are feeling safe and secure, surrounded by a loving circle of friends and family, energy begins to shift in the direction of prosperity and abundance. This is when you notice that you are moving out of the basic physiological need stage into a more comfortable place. Do you see the line between Love/Belonging and Esteem? That's where "want" begins.

Legitimate want and desire begin when you no longer need something to sustain life. When you are no longer fighting just to live. At this point, you don't need more. You want more. This is where Sarah was. This is where most of us are. We're somewhere in the upper two parts of Maslow's pyramid at the "desire-for-more" stage.

FLOWING IN THE DIRECTION OF MORE

When you are feeling good about who you are and have attained some level of achievement and satisfaction in life, you naturally begin to experience the deliciousness of wanting more. You experience this as a directional flow forward to a more prosperous and abundant life and lifestyle, filled with the variety of possessions and adventures that are your birthright. This is a style of life that is full and rich, with all cups running over (not just half full) and all cylinders firing. This is a more connected, impassioned, and complete life.

The experience of connection and the feeling of completeness are signs of your relationship with the Infinite. I call this the relationship you have with your Inner Samurai. Connection is the inner part of the *Inner* Samurai. Completeness is the *Samurai* part. Both connection and completeness are needed and represent a symbiotic relationship. To come into harmony with your desire for more is to come into harmony with your Inner Samurai.

When you are connected to your Inner Samurai, "more" easily and effortlessly flows forth. You naturally feel joyful; you are naturally excited about what you desire. You see possibilities as probabilities. That's because you are in alignment with your inner knowing, your great source of strength. Conversely, when you are disconnected from your Inner Samurai, you are caught in the illusion of separation and the stream of flow is disrupted. From this place, "lack" pours forth in the form of emotional need — the kind of need that is insatiable.

Let's go back for a moment and look at Sarah's life. Was her desire for more coming from a place of emotional need, or was it coming from her desire to flow more in the direction of prosperity and abundance? Does her desire for more money, more time, more travel, and relationships that are more loving look to you as if it is coming from a place of lack or from a place of abundance?

It's actually hard to tell sometimes because wanting more of the finer things in life has had such a bad rap for so long. Many of us have been taught that we should make due with what we have and be happy where we are. If these words sound familiar to you, then you probably grew up with the notion that wanting more is bad and being content with less is good. Or, like Sarah, that reaching a certain level or lifestyle was as far as you should go and wanting to go further was bad.

You Complete Me

Well, enough of that kind of thinking! Going further, farther, and wanting more is a natural part of who we are. We're built for more. Try it out for yourself. Think of something in the not-so-distant past that you wanted — something that actually came to pass. Maybe it was that shiny new laptop with a glossy piano black case you had your eye on, or maybe those sexy designer satin sling backs that finally went on sale. It doesn't matter what you wanted or wanted more of. Just recall what it was. How did you feel when you actually got it — actually unpacked that laptop or held the shoes in your hands? Didn't it feel great?

Then what happened? You turned on the laptop, figured out what it could do, and wanted more. Didn't you? More software, more applications, more this, more that. You put on the shoes, saw how beautiful they looked and wanted accessories to match. Without judgment or reproach, desire for more just *is*. The desire for more isn't the problem. The key is knowing the difference between being emotionally needy from lack, and flowing toward more out of prosperity and abundance.

To emotionally need something is to believe that *some external thing will complete you*. Need stems from the belief that, without something outside yourself, you are incomplete. The quintessential characteristic of emotional need is that the experience of its fulfillment is short-lived. All too soon, after achieving that which you thought you needed, you are once again thirsting, craving to feel complete.

Emotional need, flowing from incompleteness, attempts to fill a bottomless spiritual hole with material things. To emotionally need something is an expression of unhappiness. It is a statement that you do not accept your current reality and that something has to change in order for you to be happy.

The force that fuels emotional need is lack. When you are feeling lack, you have already stopped listening to the voice of your Inner Samurai. Now, instead of an inner voice, you have an inner void, which you unconsciously and endlessly attempt to fill. Here's something really important to know: No amount of physical or material stuff can ever fill this void.

Fulfillment can only come through connecting within to your Inner Samurai. When that happens, desire becomes a natural outpouring that flows in alignment with prosperity and abundance toward your natural birthright. You stop trying to fill a spiritual hole with material things. Because being connected to your Inner Samurai means that there is no hole to fill!

So, What's In Your More?

What do you think of Sarah's desire for more now? Her desire feels as if it is flowing toward prosperity, abundance, connection and completeness, doesn't it? When I showed her Maslow's *Hierarchy of Needs* and asked her where she thought she was on the pyramid, she considered this for a moment. Then she said, "I want greater intimacy with my husband, though we already have a solid relationship. I have all my basic needs covered, so I guess I'm above the need line. I'd say I'm in the esteem part of the pyramid heading toward self-actualization."

> "Yes," I affirmed, waiting to see what she would say next.
>
> "Is heading toward self-actualization and moving toward greater prosperity and abundance in life the same thing?"

"Essentially," I replied, happy to clarify. "Self-actualization and prosperity and abundance are two different models that move us in the same direction."

"Toward our natural birthright?"

"Yes."

"Toward a fuller, richer, all-cups-running-over, all-cylinders-firing life and lifestyle?" she chuckled.

I could tell she was enjoying the image this was bringing to her mind, so I smiled warmly when I said, "By Jove, Sarah, I think you've got it!"

"I do, too!"

More silence. I could tell that Sarah was processing quickly, connecting some new dots.

"Oh! So that's why I haven't been able to reach some of my goals, isn't it?" she finally said.

"Tell me more about what you're thinking," I nudged.

"I've been confusing my needs with my wants and jumping in and out of alignment with my Inner Samurai."

"Tell me more," I urged, seeing she was on to something.

"I haven't had a consistent, energetically aligned stream. Sometimes I'm connected to my Inner Samurai and sometimes I'm not. My need disconnects me from my stream of well-being, and I end up flopping around like a fish out of water."

"Yes! That's exactly what it feels like," I told her.

Now that Sarah understood what was going on, she could very quickly identify which parts of her "more" were coming from need fueled by lack and which parts were coming from the excitement of prosperity and abundance. Once we arrived at this point, we were able to get down to the business of manifesting more — something specific, something we could measure, something that Sarah could connect to through her Inner Samurai. Sarah was excited and ready to put the 60-40 Inner Samurai Rule into action.

SETTING ATTAINABLE GOALS

When Sarah and I first started working together, she was in the 30-70 zone. She came to me wanting to work on a specific financial goal for her business. Her goal was to reach the $250,000 mark by November 1, 2006. This represented a 15% revenue increase from 2005. Sarah had done her homework coming into our first meeting. She knew that her business was able to generate that type of revenue. She had been able to increase her income steadily over the past couple of years, and she had enough evidence to support that this was an attainable goal.

Sarah knew how to set realistic goals. She wasn't setting a "stretch goal"(a goal seemingly unattainable from her present resource perspective). Instead, she had come up with a tangible goal that was attainable. The only problem was . . . she was stuck. She had been hovering around the $202,000 mark for six months now. She was beginning to panic, thinking she would never reach her goal. Each time she fell behind in her daily, weekly, and monthly short-term goals she scrambled to recalibrate. She did that by increasing the amount of work she needed to do in order to meet her November deadline. She was feeling stressed, anxious, and definitely on the *need* side of the line.

Together, Sarah and I examined her goal. The first thing we did was get her some relief — we removed the arbitrary November deadline. We knew her revenue goal of $250,000 was attainable — just not by that date. Next, we looked at her financial set point.

What's Your Financial Set Point?

Sometimes people have an internal money "set point" that needs to be raised in order for them to increase their earnings. In *Secrets of the Millionaire Mind*, T. Harv Eker talks about this set point as our financial blueprint. It's something we are born with and something we can change. "It all comes down to this: if your subconscious 'financial blueprint' is not 'set' for success, nothing you learn, nothing you know, and nothing you do will make much of a difference."[1]

I was interested in finding out Sarah's financial blueprint. Was she wired for the financial success she so desired or not? First stop: Exploring what Sarah had heard about money, wealth, and rich people when she was growing up.

> "Have you ever heard the phrase, *money is the root of all evil?*" I asked.
>
> "Yes." she answered.
>
> "Did you hear it growing up?"
>
> "No."

> "Does the phrase have any meaning to you now?" I probed.
>
> "Not really," she replied.
>
> "Okay," I continued. "How about, *save your money for a rainy day; you have to work hard to make money;* or *the rich get richer while the poor get poorer?*"
>
> "Yes, yes, a little," she responded with no great amount of enthusiasm.
>
> Hmm, I thought to myself. "How about these: *We can't afford it; I'm not made of money,* or, *money doesn't grow on . . . .*"
>
> "Yes," she interrupted, sounding enthusiastic now. "Money doesn't grow on trees! My dad used to say that all the time."

And say it he did! Sarah's father didn't just *say* the phrase. He *delivered* it. With anger in his voice and a dismissive wave of his hand, Sarah's dad would heatedly stomp out of the room, effectively putting an end to any and all further discussion about money.

> "Think that has anything to do with your money mind-set?" I asked.
>
> "Yes," she said.
>
> "What do you think your father's words and actions were saying about his relationship with money?"
>
> "That, when my father couldn't pay for things my sister and I were asking for, he blamed us for what he saw as his inability to make enough money to provide for us." Sarah contemplated that new insight for a moment. "There always

was a cap for him on what he thought he could earn. Only he knew what that cap was. We never did, he felt stuck, too, just like me. He got angry at us for his financial mind-set."

Bingo! Sarah had discovered the heart of what was subconsciously governing her financial set point. We had now identified two things keeping Sarah from reaching her financial goal:

- Sarah's relationship with her Inner Samurai
- Sarah's subconscious financial set point

Everybody Needs Some Money, Sometime

One of the best ways to increase your financial set point is to change subconscious imprinting through verbal programming. Sarah jumped into this task with great enthusiasm. First, she wrote down every statement she could remember hearing from her parents, extended family, and friends of the family. Then she expanded her sphere of influence to include what she picked up from TV, radio, and magazines. Finally, she thought about what she heard from her teachers, people in her church, and even what her friends repeated from their parents. Within a week, Sarah had a complete list of phrases, words, and statements she had picked up about money, wealth, and rich people.

Next, we explored how Sarah believed those statements had affected her financial life, so far. Sarah had some interesting perspectives. "I've been saving for a rainy day all my life, and what has that brought me? Fear of the future. Fear of not having enough."

Do you think that had anything to do with Sarah's inability to reach her revenue goal? You bet it did! Her revenue goal was based on a desire to spend money on herself and her family. It was never about saving. This was flying smack-dab in the face of a tape that had been playing in her subconscious for a very long time. A tape she never knew existed!

> "What other insights have you come to?" I asked.
>
> "Having money means you're somebody. One of the reasons I want $250,000 is to prove to others and myself that I'm not just a pretty face dependent upon my husband to support me."

Sarah became engaged to Gary in her senior year at Sarah Lawrence. Right after college, she moved back home, planned her wedding, and got married within the year. Sarah had never lived on her own. She'd never provided financially for herself. She had never been financially independent. No wonder her $250K revenue goal meant so much to her! She was tired of being financially dependent on others. She had tied financial dependence in with her feelings of self-worth, self-importance, and value as a person. Attaining her revenue goal meant more to her than just an increase in income. It meant freedom.

It was both a relief and a surprise for Sarah to see how much this goal meant to her, on so many different levels. Still, she was pumped up. She was ready to make some changes.

> "Sarah, are you willing for your story to change?" I now asked.

"Yes!"

"Are you ready to adopt a millionaire mindset?"

"Uhhhh," she hesitated, "I don't know."

"Are you ready for *that* story to change?"

"Yes!"

"Okay, let's begin to tip things in your favor by applying the 60-40 Inner Samurai Rule. What's one action you can put into effect, today and every day, toward your $250K revenue goal?"

Sarah thought a moment, then blurted out, "I can have a millionaire mind set!"

I chuckled and told her that she was in good company. T. Harv Eker uses a similar statement with his clients. He has them place their hand over their heart and say, "What I heard about money isn't necessarily true. I choose to adopt new ways of thinking that support my happiness and success." Then he has them touch their head and say, "I have a millionaire mind set." She tried it a few times grinning from ear to ear. "This feels right. This feels good," she kept repeating.

Now Sarah was aligning with her Inner Samurai. She was ready to put 60% of her action toward her goal in the now. Sarah was primed for success.

SUCCESS, THE BATTLE FOR DOMINANCE

There are plenty of things you can do to achieve success, although, if you have unconscious negative beliefs about success, none of them will work. And it's not just about your beliefs, but also about what society believes and what your parents believed and wanted for you. It always comes back around to our parents doesn't it?

Sarah grew up in a sleeper community right outside New Haven, Connecticut. Her father commuted every day to work on the train to New York City, while her mother stayed home to take care of Sarah and her little sister. Dad made good money. He was proud of the fact that he could take care of his family without the need for his wife to work outside the home. He left early in the morning, before Sarah got up, and returned late at night, often missing dinner with the family. According to Sarah, Dad's definition of success had to do with owning his own home, taking care of his family's financial needs, being able to afford vacations, putting his daughters through college, and making sure they married the right kind of men. This meant that they would marry men just like him — men who would take care of them.

Sarah's mother's definition of success was making sure her children were brought up properly, that they were neat and clean, and that they knew their manners and behaved appropriately when they went out to the country club for Sunday dinner. Together, Sarah's mom and dad complemented each other's definition of success, and so the family hummed along nicely from year to year.

Growing up in an affluent and upwardly mobile society, Sarah's friends reinforced her parents' ideal of success. They all went to church. They all wore designer clothes, hung out at the country club, and got good grades. All Sarah's friends had plans to go to college. Everyone had a boyfriend. No one was having sex, or, if they were, they didn't dare talk about it. Moreover, everyone acted the *good girl* part.

True to their definition of success, Sarah's parents sent her away to the college of her — and their — choice. While at Sarah Lawrence, Sarah studied art history, earned good grades, joined Alpha Chi Omega, and met Gary. After college, she married and had children, just like her mom. Her husband didn't want her to work, but for a while she volunteered as a museum docent. She later worked part-time as a curator for a small up-and-coming gallery. She liked making money to spend on a few extra things. She also found that she liked making decisions and she liked the respect she received for quickly being able to spot high quality art. Sarah dreamed of one day being a gallery owner. Then she had her first baby and she let her dream fade away.

Three children and 20 years later, Sarah came back around to her dream. With her eye for spotting high quality art, and with the financial help of her husband, she opened a posh gallery and went into business for herself. Gary and her children couldn't have been happier for her — as long as her new business didn't interfere with running the house, attending Gary's social functions, and the children's games and recitals. This meant that Sarah kept to a rigorous and structured schedule in order to do it all. She told herself that she was glad to do it because it meant that she had her family along with her independence and freedom. Sarah's entrepreneurial spirit was alive and doing well, even if she was tired all the time.

From Chrysalis to Butterfly

Nevertheless, there was a problem. Sarah's definition of success was clashing with Gary's definition of success. The definition of success she had grown up with had evolved. Sure, she still wanted the home in the suburbs, the country club membership, and a college education for her children. However, she now thought in terms of her and Gary co-providing for the family. She thought her business and the work Gary was doing were equally important. Most disturbingly to Gary and the children, she was now talking about everyone doing their fair share around the house. She even suggested they hire someone to clean for them.

Sarah wanted more. And that *more* didn't fit in with her husband's definition of success. He struggled to understand. What had happened to the Sarah he knew and liked? What had happened to the woman he married? Nothing and everything. At her Inner Samurai core Sarah was still the same woman she had always been, though her outer self was now unfolding to reflect her true knowing. She was less concerned with pleasing others and more in tune with knowing what pleased her. She was less anxious about what others thought of her and more interested in what she thought of herself. Sarah was metamorphosing into a colorful, spirited butterfly. Sarah was excited about emerging! Gary, on the other hand, was less than enthusiastic.

Sarah still was a loving wife and mother. In fact, those were two of the things she enjoyed being the most. However, that was not all she wanted to be. She also wanted to be a businessperson and have a successful career. In addition, she wanted to do a few extra things, beyond the role of wife and mother; things that would enrich her life. Gary loved Sarah and wanted her to be happy. He understood how rewarding it was to be successful outside the home. The only thing was, he wanted Sarah to be happy in the old way he was familiar with, rather than this new, threatening way. "Why can't the old Sarah come back?" Gary asked his wife a thousand times.

Sarah's and Gary's definitions of success were out of sync with each other. Gary blamed Sarah for upsetting the apple cart. Sarah accused Gary of being old fashioned. Gary was happy with things just the way they were. Sarah was desperate for change. She was spending time thinking about how to get things to happen the way she wanted them to be. She was in the 30-70 zone, trying to force outcomes. She was far away from the effortless action of the 60-40 Inner Samurai Rule.

Did this have anything to do with Sarah's apparent lack of success in getting to her $250K revenue goal? Yes, it did! The farther she moved away from the 60-40 tipping point, the farther she was away from her place of power, her Inner Samurai. The more plans she set into motion that were about pushing away what she didn't want rather than moving toward what she did want, the farther she was from having what she wanted in the now. Sarah was feeling stressed. Gary was feeling worried.

STRESS, YOUR INNER SAMURAI'S WARNING BELL

Your Inner Samurai communicates with you in a recognizable voice. It is always calm, centered, and strong. The further away you go from that voice, the more uneasy you feel. The more uneasy you feel, the worse your experience is. The worse the experience, the more confused, frustrated, and stressed you become. Sound like resistance to you? Bingo! Stress is your Inner Samurai's warning bell of how close you are getting to the wall of resistance, and how far away you are from the 60-40 comfort zone.

Before you feel full-blown stress, you will feel a slight discomfort, something you can easily ignore. This discomfort is telling you that you are out of the 60-40 zone and have, in fact, moved past the 50-50 mark. Once you reach the 40-60 zone, you may feel anxious, apprehensive, and concerned. You may feel as if you need to do something, though you don't know what. At this point, it is important to heed the warning bell. Listen to the voice of your Inner Samurai. It is calling you to turn in the opposite direction, to return home. (Most people ignore this calling.)

Once you move into the 30-70 zone, you will feel extremely uncomfortable. This is the level psychologists label as actual stress. Stress is synonymous with worry. If you are worried, you are in a state of stress. To your body, stress is synonymous with change. Anything that causes a change in your life causes stress. It doesn't matter if it is a positive change or a negative change; change is stressful to the body.

By the time you hit the 20-80 mark, you are so far away from your centered, inner knowing that your Inner Samurai is putting out an even louder warning bell, one that psychologists call "overstress." Depression, anxiety attacks, and insomnia are all symptoms of overstress. This is generally the point where people start self-medicating with alcohol, food, gambling, or drugs.

Can you pinpoint which zone Sarah and Gary were in? Were they feeling stressed or overstressed? If you said stressed, you are correct. Though they were manifesting it differently, they were both in the 30-70 zone. Both Sarah's and Gary's Inner Samurais were doing a great job of getting their attention. You could almost hear their Inner Samurais trying to help them find their way. Similar to the voice of a car navigational system, you could almost hear their Inner Samurais saying, "At the next intersection, please make a legal U-turn." The Inner Samurai always sends the same message during times of stress: "Stop what you are doing, turn in the opposite direction, and come back home."

After lots of conversation, Sarah and Gary decided to explore their ideas of success together. More significantly, they decided to align their definitions of success with their inner knowers. Sarah began applying, in earnest, the 60-40 Inner Samurai Rule to her life as well as her $250K revenue goal. She turned goal setting into an art and had great results with it. She soon set a new goal of making sure 70% of her action was taken today, in the now, in the red-hot minute, with only 30% of her action taken in the future.

Gary turned out to be her greatest champion. After working through his own issues surrounding success and money, he quickly became Sarah's strongest advocate for joyous creation. Now their family life is flourishing, Sarah's business and Gary's work are prospering, and both are contributing equally to the kind of life and lifestyle they want to live.

And that goal of $250K? Goal, schmoal. Sarah passed that a long time ago.

NOTES FROM YOUR INNER SAMURAI

I have met brave women who are exploring the outer edge of human possibility, with no history to guide them, and with a courage to make themselves vulnerable and I find that moving beyond words.

— Gloria Steinem

- For success in goal setting, follow the 60-40 Inner Samurai Rule. Take 60% of your action toward your goal today with only 40% of your action remaining for the future.

- Become familiar with the difference between emotional need and flowing in the direction of more. Need comes from a place of scarcity and lack. Flowing in the direction of more feels like movement toward prosperity and abundance.

- Get intimate with your Inner Samurai to savor the experience of connection and the feeling of completeness.

- Set attainable goals that you know you can accomplish. Then follow the 60-40 Inner Samurai Rule to achieve them.

- Take an inventory of all the words and phrases you heard about money, wealth, and rich people when you were growing up. This will help you determine your subconscious financial set point and give you a tangible place to start if you want to increase it.

- Recall what your parents' definition of success was — for them and for you — growing up. This information is often fraught with hidden land mines thwarting your success in the now.

- Compare your parent's definition of success with your definition of success. Then adopt your own.

- Get really good at hearing your Inner Samurai's warning bell the minute it sounds. This one thing will save your life.

Chapter 10

SCAPEGOATS EXTRAORDINAIRE: TIME AND MONEY

INNER SAMURAI PRIORITY AND VALUE SYSTEMS

We can tell our values by looking at our checkbook stubs.

— Gloria Steinem

Poor, poor time and money. Don't you feel sorry for them? Every time you look around, time and money are being blamed for one more thing. We blame time for the reason we don't start a new venture or finish a project. We blame money when we don't try something we're interested in, go someplace we want to go, or have the possessions we desire. There are simply no other two words in the English language that are blamed more often than the twins: time and money.

Plans are changed, cancelled, and rescheduled because we run out of or need more time. "I didn't have time," we complain, when we can't get something done. "There wasn't enough time," we whine, when a deadline is missed. "I don't know if I'll have time to do that," we warn someone, when he or she asks us to do something. We either don't have any time, don't have enough time, or don't know if we will have time. What's happened to time? Has it gone somewhere?

On the flip side, sometimes we have too much time. Things take too long. Minutes drag by. Sometimes, even, time stops. "It took forever to get here," we sigh when we're late. "Are we there yet?" our children drone from the back seat of the car. "The moment I saw you, time stood still," lovers declare in amazement. Time is most remarkable. It has the ability to slow down, speed up, stretch, and bend. It can fly by and stop dead in its tracks. What an amazing thing time is. All hail the powerful time!

Money, too, has these same attributes. We either don't have enough money or have way too much of it. Wait. What's the problem with having too much money? Well, have you ever tried to get financial aid for college if your parents make too much money? Or had to deal with requests for money if you've come into an inheritance or have just won the lottery? Too much money can indeed be a problem.

However, most people see themselves as being on the "not enough" side of money. "Gosh, I'd love to do that, but I can't afford it," we say when we think we can't do something. "Are you kidding? We're not spending that kind of money on *that*!" we admonish when we think something costs too much. "Let's just take a couple of weekend trips," we compromise when we think money is tight.

We let money, like time, control us. We make money and time into something they are not. We make the twins, time and money, into our universal scapegoats.

A Brief History of Scapegoating

Have you ever wondered where the word *scapegoat* came from? I was curious about its origins, so I looked it up. It turns out that *scapegoating* has some pretty interesting history.

The first reference to the word *scapegoat* is found in the Old Testament. In Leviticus, we read of a sacrificial goat being driven off into the wilderness on Yom Kippur. On this Jewish Day of Atonement, Aaron, son of Moses, is instructed to bring a live goat before the altar and:

> Lay both his hands upon the head of the live goat, confess over him all the iniquities of the people of Israel, and all their transgressions, all their sins; and he shall put them up onto the head of the goat and send him away into the wilderness by the hand of a man who is in readiness. The goat shall bear all their iniquities upon him to a solitary land; and he shall let the goat go in the wilderness.[1]

The Tyndale translation of the Bible, published in 1526 by English religious reformer William Tyndale, was the first Bible to be mass-produced, thanks to the invention of the printing press in 1440. It was here that the word *scapegoat* was first used in mass print. Because of this, Tyndale is usually given credit — correctly or incorrectly — for the forming of the word. There is also some disagreement among Biblical scholars as to whether Tyndale's use of the term may have been a mistranslation.

Even if it was a mistranslation, mass production now made corrections to manuscripts too costly. So the term "scapegoat" stayed in Tyndale's Bible. The use of the word was furthered in 1611 in The King James version.

It wasn't until the early part of the 19th century that the figurative, secular use of the word *scapegoat* turned up in non-religious writings. *Scapegoat* (and the verb *scapegoating*) came to mean: a person, often innocent, who is blamed and punished for the sins, crimes, or sufferings of others.

Doesn't that sound a lot like the twins? The twins: time and money?

So, Whose Time Is It?

My client Rebecca was guilty of scapegoating time. We'd have a fantastic coaching session together, make a lot of headway on her business plan, and then nothing would be done between sessions. Alternatively, she would scramble to get something done the day of our meeting, sending me an apologetic email saying, "Sorry to get this to you so late; I just ran out of time." Then, we'd meet for our call, have another great coaching session together, and the cycle of coaching sessions followed by no further progress continued.

Have you ever had this happen to you? (Hand up in the air for me.) You have the best intentions in the world, are fired up, jazzed, and raring to go about something. Then, other things start getting in the way. First, it's the kids. Next, it's the laundry. Then it's work. And don't forget the cookies that need to be baked, the car that needs to be fixed, or the closet that can't wait another minute to be organized. Pretty soon, a week has gone by. And the very thing you were so excited about doing still sits, waiting.

You feel guilty about not getting around to it and resolve that you will do it — just as soon as you feed the fish, walk the dog, and pick up the dry cleaning. Three weeks go by, and this thing that originally made you so energized has now become a "project." Something to put on your to-do list. Something that *needs* to be done. This thing, once so wonderful, has become a task hanging over your head. Something you need to get off your plate. A burden.

> "What happened?" I asked Rebecca, after she, once again, hadn't gotten around to her coaching assignment.
>
> "I don't know. I guess life just happened. I was all revved up about it, but then things just got in the way. I've always had a big problem with procrastinating."
>
> "Ah, procrastination," I said. "So this is something that has happened to you a lot?"
>
> "Yes! All the time. I get so excited about something, and then I just can't seem to follow through."

Does this sound like you? It used to sound like me. I was famous for procrastinating and doing things at the last minute. That was until I figured out *whose time it was*.

How much time is there in a day? One day. There are 24 hours. That's 1,440 minutes or 86,400 seconds. That's how much time I have in a day. That's how much time you have in a day, too. I have the same amount of time as everyone else. I have the same time as Mrs. Klein, my elderly neighbor, who always manages to bring around to all her neighbors a quart of soup in the fall, a mason jar of homemade strawberry jam in the summer, and thumbprint cookies at Christmas. I have the same amount of time as my business associate Michele, whose turn-around time on getting transcriptions back to me is impressive. I have the same amount of time as Donald Trump who, if you've ever read his books, seems to get more done in a week then I do in a year.

So what sets us apart? Is it time? Does Mrs. Klein have more time than I do? Does Donald Trump have more time to do things because he has a staff of hundreds? I doubt it. Having more people working for you doesn't give you more time; it just changes the way you spend your time. So what makes some people use time efficiently and other people procrastinate? I can tell you one thing. Time is not the culprit.

It's Never About Time

People continue to think it's about time. Really, though, it's about our relationship with ourselves. It's about what's important to you and what's important to me. To Mrs. Klein, it's important to her that she gets her strawberries picked, canned, and distributed early in the summer. To Michele, it's about being true to her word. One of the reasons I hired her was because she said she could and would turn things back around to me quickly. To Donald Trump, it's all about making a deal. And he makes a lot of them. To him, time is money, so he makes good use of his time.

What do all three of these people have in common? They are in control of their time. They don't let anyone or anything stand in the way of doing what they want to do. They don't scapegoat time. Whether it's making sure that everyone has cookies for Christmas, that a contract goes out in the mail by Monday, or that a corporate research and development team meets on Thursday, each of these people knows that they are in control of time. Time is not in control of them.

"Yeah . . . but," I can hear you saying (I, too, used to say this to myself), "you don't understand. Little Joey fell, broke his arm, and needed to be rushed to the emergency room." Sure, I completely understand when these things come up. Life happens, as Rebecca said. Still, and here's the point, you are in control of what you do with your time and how you spend it. All 86,400 seconds of it. Of course, there is no question that you will rush little Joey to the emergency room, sit with him, hold him, and love on him afterward. I'd do, and have done, the same.

It's not the occasional emergency that trips us up. It's what we've been doing with the other 1,440 minutes of our time before the emergency comes along. If we've been in control of our time all along, we are free to be fully present when an emergency arises. It's never about time. It's about our relationship with ourselves. Specifically, in relation to time, it's about our priorities.

Little Joey falling out of a tree, breaking his arm, and needing to be rushed to the hospital is an in-the-moment priority. An A-1 priority. It isn't something to be put off until later. How about your laundry? Cleaning the closet? Finishing that one last thing before you start on the thing you really want to do? Where's your priority there? What about the rest of your time?

Getting Real About What's Important

When I first started working with my business coach setting up my new business, I had not fully accepted responsibility for my time. Like Rebecca, I would have terrific sessions with my coach, feel energized with the progress we were making, and swear I was going to get something done. Then, well . . . I wouldn't get anything done. I tried every time management and planning trick I knew. I'd put something I wanted to do on my to-do list, block out time during my day to work on it, break it into smaller tasks, set timers, and say affirmations. I got up early, went to bed late, and allocated it to my most active, productive time of the day. I still didn't get around to starting (let alone finishing) that thing I was so excited about. Oh, don't get me wrong. Sometimes I would get things done. And boy, did that feel great! Most of the time, though, I'd get my assignments done in fits and spurts. I was inconsistent.

"You don't understand," I moaned one day to my coach, "My father is dying, and I'm his primary caregiver. I never know what's going to come up. I'm not in control of my time." What she said in response floored me. "Well, Susan, maybe you just aren't serious about getting your new business up and running." Not serious! Are you kidding? I was very serious! I had been on fire about getting my new business up and running ever since my Momacita passed away six months earlier. Whatever in the world was my business coach talking about? Wasn't a dying loved one a good enough reason not to have gotten something done?

I was angry. I re-doubled my efforts. I began getting up even earlier to get my assignments done. I'd run upstairs to the library to work on the computer while my dad was napping. I'd bring my notes with me when I went to the drugstore to pick up his prescriptions, just in case I had time to work on them while waiting for the order to be filled. I even began carrying around a mini-cassette recorder when I walked in the morning, to capture my ideas.

Of course, every single time my dad would call my name, I would gladly stop whatever I was doing and go to his side. I never had a moment's hesitation, never a question. I loved spending time with my dad. He was easy to care for. We'd always had a terrific relationship, one that my girlfriends all wished they had with their dads. I felt it both an honor and a privilege to be a part of his death and dying process. I felt called to do it. In fact, the main reason I moved from South Dakota to Virginia was to be within easy driving distance of my parents. When my Momacita passed away, it seemed natural for me to become my dad's primary caregiver.

Right after she passed away, Dad was still able to care for himself. He drove, dressed himself, went out to dinner with friends, and continued his caseload as an expert psychological witness for the states of West Virginia and Pennsylvania. Then, during the summer when he was diagnosed with myeloma (a type of cancer) in addition to his leukemia, he became less able to do the things he once did. By August, he had resigned as an expert witness. In September he went into surgery — the doctors took one look and closed him up. By mid-September, I had moved my base of operation from my home in Virginia to my dad's home near Pittsburgh, Pennsylvania.

The time I spent caring for him during the last four months of his life was extraordinary. As I spent more and more time caring for him, my time spent working on my business became less and less. Then one evening it dawned on me, as Dad and I were watching a re-run of *Gunsmoke* together: I would rather be watching *Gunsmoke* with my dad than doing anything else in the world. This was it. Nothing else mattered. Holding hands, sharing companionable silence, and wondering how Marshal Dillon and Festus would deal with the latest Dodge City crime caper was exactly where I wanted to be. I had plenty of time to focus on my business later. This, I knew, was the last amount of time Dad and I would ever spend together on this earth. Spending time with him was my A-1 priority. Everything else paled in contrast.

Does It or Doesn't It, The Only Question Worth Asking

Walking to my bedroom that evening, I knew something had shifted. I felt it, from within. I knew I had aligned with my inner knowing. I knew I was in alignment with my inner priority system. With my Inner Samurai. Life was happening. My dad was dying. I was done with splitting my energy between caring for him, starting up my new business, freelancing as a conductor, and getting things in order before his passing. I was finished with time controlling me. It was time for me to take control of my 1,440 minutes of the day. It was time for me to state my priorities and line-up with them — to be aligned with my Inner Samurai Priority System.

Sleep came easily for me that night. It was a nice relief. My inner calm had been restored. And even though I was awakened several times during the night with, "Suzy, would you please come here?" I felt rested in the morning. I felt sure. I was ready to take action.

> The first thing I did was tell my dad, "You are my number one priority. Everything else will take care of itself."
>
> He protested, "What about your new business?"
>
> "That can wait."
>
> "What about conducting?"
>
> "I'll fulfill what contracts I already have and not accept any more while you are alive."
>
> Then came his inevitable practical question. "What about money?"
>
> "No prob, Dad. I have investments and savings that will see me through. Besides, money always comes easily to me." He smiled. Later that week he wrote me a check. When I began to object, he waved me off with, "Here's one way money is coming to you." We both smiled. My inner Samurai smiled, too.

The next thing I did was call my business coach to tell her my decision and work out an arrangement where I could postpone my coaching sessions with her. She was amenable. Then, I called my web designer and told her the same thing. She, too, was very understanding about my decision. After that, I called a few conductor friends of mine and arranged for them to be on stand-by to cover some of my later-in-the-year conducting gigs if something should happen to Dad. I sent them scores and let the people who had hired me know the situation. Everyone was fantastic about working with me, now that I had clearly stated my priority.

Finally, I sat down with Dad again and said, "I think it's time to get Hospice involved."

There is such power in being clear about what's important to you. Knowing what's important not only defines your priorities, it also gives you a basis from which you can determine what to say yes to and when to say no. Once you have your priorities in place, then the only question to ask yourself is, "Does this or doesn't this activity support my priority?"

Top Two Priorities, One Month Commitment

Let's return to my coaching client, Rebecca. When I asked her what her top two priorities were for the present month, she was quick to respond.

> "Being a great mom to my kids and getting my business plan done."
>
> "Okay, great! Let's get more specific. If you could wave a realistic magic wand, how would you be as a great mom to your children?"
>
> Rebecca thought for a moment, then said, "I'd be present, fresh, and there for them when they came home from school. I'd take them to the park to play on weekends. I'd walk with them to swim lessons and stay

there watching, without answering my cell phone. I'd be involved with their homework assignments, instead of just asking them if they'd gotten them done. I'd be fully present when I read them their bedtime stories and not skip any pages. We'd have a good time making chocolate chip cookies together on weekends."

Rebecca had a great list of things she would do with her children this month, given they were one of her top two priorities. Best yet, when she talked about the things she would do and how she would be, there was an inner warmth and glow in her voice. I could tell she was connected with her Inner Samurai Priority System. Nothing in her list felt like a *should, ought,* or *must*. I also noticed that the mundane tasks of running a household were absent.

"Rebecca, does it seem realistic that you will complete your business plan?"

"Yes!"

"How can you say yes so emphatically?"

"Because I only have two priorities this month!"

Bingo! That's the key. Two priorities; one-month commitment. That's all. Of course, if you can, you might narrow that priority down to one. Most of us, though, unless we are in an extreme situation, will have two. A one-month commitment to two priorities is achievable. With only three remaining parts of her business plan to go, Rebecca certainly could finish it this month and still have plenty of time to spend with her other priority — her children.

Then the voice inside her head began to kick in.

"What about the laundry?"

"Does getting the laundry done support or get in the way of either one of your priorities?" I asked her.

"Yes . . . No. I mean, I want them to have clean clothes to wear. I just can't go all month without doing laundry!"

I chuckled, imagining a month's worth of dirty t-shirts and socks waiting to be washed in stacks outside the laundry room. "Yes, of course do the laundry. After — not before — you've attended to your top two priorities."

"Oh. So that would be the same for dishes, going shopping, the contract work gigs I'm doing, and committees I'm serving on at school and church?"

"Yes. Being a great mom to your kids and getting your business plan done are your A-1 priorities for this month. Let nothing and no one get in the way of them."

At first, this was a difficult task for Rebecca. She was so used to another way of being. Changing to be in alignment with her Inner Samurai Priority System was a challenge. Yet, she persevered. One week later, she reported that she had been able to clear her mind and her desk by the time her children came home from school, so she could greet them with a genuine smile, ready to spend time and be with them. She also completed the one-year objectives section of her business plan. When I asked her how she managed to stay focused, she said, "I kept asking myself that one question: *Does this or doesn't this activity support my priority?* The answer was immediately clear. Then all I had to do was move in that direction."

At the end of one month, Rebecca completed her business plan. She was ecstatic! She was pleased with what she had accomplished. She had also done every one of the things she said she wanted to do with and for her children. She felt good about herself, her relationship to herself, and all that she had accomplished. Best yet, Rebecca learned, not through reading a book, but by direct application, that she could control time. She now knew that she, not time, was in control. Moreover, she did that simply and easily by assigning two priorities each month that were in line with her Inner Samurai Priority System.

Now it's your turn. What are your two priorities this month? What are the two things that you are most passionate about doing? Notice I didn't say the two things you think you should do. What are the two things you are jazzed about and excited to do? If you are feeling passionate, joyful, excited, eager, energized, and inwardly charged to do them, then you can bet you are in alignment with your Inner Samurai Priority System. And you know what that means? You're aligned with your greatest knower, your Source, and your strength. You're in the now place of power. So, go for it. Then email me. I'd love to know how this month went for you.

It's Never About Money

If it's never about money, then what is it about, exactly? Like time, money is about our relationship with ourselves. Time's particular emphasis is on priorities to self — what we define as important to us. Money's particular emphasis is on values to self — what we find of value to us. The Gloria Steinem quote at the start of this chapter says it all: "We can tell our values by looking at our checkbook stubs."

During the spring of 2007, I began looking around for a new business coach who would help me take my business to the next level — that of consultant. I defined what I wanted in a coach, gathered recommendations from my satisfied coaching and consulting colleagues, and began researching possible candidates. Each time I found someone I particularly liked, I set up a coaching consultation call with him or her and engaged the person in a dialogue about my new business direction. During this process, I met some wonderful coaches. Then there was this one coach I called who specialized in helping coaches become consultants.

At the end of our call together, I asked him how much his services were. He didn't hesitate.

> "I require a year commitment at $1,500 per month."

I burst out laughing. I could understand the year commitment. I could see the value of staying with a coaching consultant for that long a period.

> But . . . ,"*Fifteen hundred dollars*? You've got to be kidding!" I said.
>
> "Oh, so I see you're uncomfortable with that amount of money."
>
> "No! Not at all! $1,500 isn't a problem for me."
>
> "Well, I offer a 10% discount for anyone who signs up for a year, so that might help."

I wondered if he hadn't heard me say that money wasn't the issue.

> "Listen, it's not the money. I'm okay with the money."

"You know, Susan, lots of people have issues with money."

Geez, this guy really wasn't listening.

"Yes, I'm sure you're right. In my case, however, that's not what I'm laughing about."

I paused. I wanted so badly for him to ask me what I was laughing about. Wouldn't you want to know? Apparently, he didn't. I waited — I'm good with silence over the phone so it became a stand off. Seconds ticked by. He still didn't ask.

"Okay," he acquiesced. "I'll bite. What is it?"

"Here's what I know," I said. "It's never about money. It's about value." Silence. "In your case, I just haven't heard anything that tells me that you will be offering me fifteen hundred dollars worth of value."

He defended his price by reminding me that his products and services had stood the test of time, how many satisfied clients he had, and how they had all gone on to make it big as consultants.

"That's great. I'm glad those folks all had such success. Pay attention now, though. *I* don't see fifteen hundred dollars worth of value in what you are offering. For *me*."

He seemed a little taken aback by that. "No one's ever said that to me before."

"I bet they haven't. I bet they said they couldn't afford $1,500, didn't they?"

"Yes."

"That's what most of us say when we believe it's about money. In reality, it's not about money. It's about value."

We soon signed off. At the end of our conversation, he thanked me for my candor and wished me all the best. I wished him the same and went on with my search. Six months later, he sent me an email.

"You know," he wrote, "I've been thinking a lot about what you said about value, and you're right. I'm not really offering my clients fifteen hundred dollars worth of value. I'm asking them for $1,500 worth of money. There's a big difference between offering value and asking for money, isn't there?"

"Yes," I confirmed. "One comes from an energetic place of lack; the other from abundance."

"That's what I thought. Would you be open to doing some executive coaching with me?"

How Much Value Is In Your Pocket?

It's never about money, friends. It's about what value you see in something. Let's test this out. What would you pay $1,500 for? Translation — what would fifteen hundred dollars buy that would be of value to you? Maybe a month's worth of rent or mortgage on your apartment or home? Perhaps it would be a Disney World vacation with your family, a new computer, or money placed in a college fund account. What constitutes fifteen hundred dollars of value to you? To *you*. Not to anyone else. Fifteen hundred dollars of value to one person will surely be different to another. Once you can answer this question, then you know the most important thing about money — it's all about value.

Doesn't it feel so much better to think about money in that way? Now, when you go to the store, instead of spending $85 on groceries, select the items that will go into your shopping cart based on their value to you. Does buying something on sale appeal to you? Don't buy it because it is cheaper (notice how that energy feels). Rather, buy it because the sale price is in alignment with its value. Line up with the *value*, and money will increase. Line up with the *price* of something, and money will decrease. Subtle difference? Not to your Inner Samurai. Your Inner Samurai is energetically aligned. Your Inner Samurai is all about value.

What's in your pocket? Never leave home without it. Leave home without what? Why, your Inner Samurai Value System, of course!

NOTES FROM YOUR INNER SAMURAI

People first, then money, then things.

— Suze Orman

- Cultivate a great relationship with yourself. Time and money will thank you.

- Stop blaming time and money for not having or being able to do what you want. Instead, be honest with yourself about your priorities and values.

- Keep others informed about your priorities and values. This way, you will have eliminated the need to do things you don't want to do and won't have to explain to others why.

- The next time you hear yourself saying, "There just aren't enough hours in the day . . . ," stop. Then remind yourself of your two A-1 priorities for the month, and ask yourself, *does this or doesn't this activity support my priority?*

- Be guided by your Inner Samurai Priority System. She will never steer you wrong.

- You get to decide how you will spend your time. We all have the same 24 hours, or 1,440 minutes, or 86,400 seconds in each day. Enjoy them!

- Buy value, not cost. Knowing the difference between $1,500 and fifteen hundred dollars worth of value is priceless.

- Never leave home without it . . . your Inner Samurai Value System, of course!

Chapter 11

CONNECT TO GIVE, NOT CONNECT TO GET

YOUR INNER SAMURAI'S PERSPECTIVE ON NETWORKING AND SELLING

Networking is simply the cultivating of mutually beneficial, give and take, win-win relationships. It works best, however, when emphasizing the 'give' part.

— Bob Burg

This chapter could have just as easily been named, *Give to Give, Not Sell to Get*. I also might have called it, *Give to Give, Not Give to Get*. Though those titles would have been fine, neither of them would have spoken to the heart of what Inner Samurai business is all about. Neither title was inclusive enough to encapsulate fully what running your business from the inside out really means.

An Inner Samurai business is different from any other kind of business. At its base is the precisely crafted term, Inner Samurai. Two words — *inner* and *samurai*. Each of these words is fine alone. Putting these two words together, though, increases their "wow factor" by a quantum factor of ten.

Generally speaking, neither one of these words is capitalized outside the context of this book, unless you see them at the start of a sentence. *Samurai* is a noun. A common noun describing a class of people — the hereditary warrior class in feudal Japan. As such, samurai is not a proper noun naming a specific person, place, or thing.

Inner is an adjective. An adjective precedes and modifies a noun or a pronoun with describing, identifying, or quantifying words. In this case, *inner* pertains to the spiritual aspect of samurai. When combined, the two words form a proper noun, or proper name representing a unique entity. Inner Samurai — proper together, common alone.

I Hate Networking and Sales

This is the number one complaint I hear from my clients. Just saying the words networking and sales has elicited many an involuntary sigh from even my most outgoing, ambitious clients. Say those words at an entrepreneurial conference and you can count on three things happening. First: Silence. Silence is quickly followed by, "I know you're right; we really should," accompanied by nods and murmurs of agreement, and then a swift change of topic.

Why is this? Is it because the words *networking* and *sales* bring up the image of high-pressured salespeople and glad-handing exchanges of business cards? Or, maybe these words bring to mind those uncomfortable moments at networking events when

Connect to Give, Not Connect to Get
Your Inner Samurai's Perspective on Networking and Selling
Ch. 11

someone asks you, without really meaning it, "So, tell me a little bit about your business?"

Maybe it's the thought of projected sales quotes, cold-calling, or generating leads that makes these words so unpalatable. To give this networking and sales thing a fair shake, however, I do know of some people who absolutely love to network and sell. In fact, one of my oldest and dearest friends loves to sell. When Sam and I talk on the phone, his excitement and enthusiasm for sales is so genuine, I just have to smile.

Sam is an expert at selling. He's received so many Salesman-of-the-Year awards, it's hard even for him to keep track. Sam loves to sell. He makes selling look easy. Over the years, he was so successful at networking and sales that he quickly achieved Vice President of Sales of a major U.S. manufacturing firm.

Sam is a classy guy. Not at all the kind of slimy salesperson you might picture when you think of sales. One day I asked him, "What's your secret? What makes you so good at networking and sales?" His eyes mischievously sparkled as he leaned in close. He looked both ways, merrily casting about to make sure no one was listening to the great secret he was about to disclose. Then he said, "It's never about selling, Susan. It's about connecting to people and forming relationships with them. The same is true for networking. It's never about being seen, it's about seeing others."

In 1942, Leonard Bernstein, famous American composer and conductor, wrote *I Hate Music: A Cycle of Five Kids' Songs for Soprano and Piano*. The music is wittily written from the perspective of children, yet these songs are challenging to sing and play. "I Hate Music" is third in the five-cycle set and begins: "I hate music! But I like to sing." I think the same could be said about Sam. He hates selling, but he likes to connect.

WOMANING — WOMAN AS A VERB

One of the things that women do well is build relationships. Women like to connect. Women like to find common ground and mutual points of interest. When they do, they settle in, happy to begin the process of going deep. I have a name for this process of going deep: *womaning*. It's a term I use to describe the way that women like to get to know each other. Womaning is partly about interest, partly about curiosity, and all about connection. Women want to know about you. They want to see you. They want to touch you — perhaps not physically, but emotionally. Used in this context, womaning is a verb — an action verb. When a woman is womaning, she is connecting and building relationships.

One of the most fun encounters I've had with womaning was when I attended a workshop called "Kabbalah and Dzogchen" with Rabbi David Cooper at the Omega Center in Rhinebeck, New York, in June of 2007. I missed the Friday evening get-to-know-you session. When I showed up Saturday morning everyone was curious about who the new girl was. For the most part, the men smiled and were cordial, offered to get me situated with pillows and folding floor seats, since I had elected to sit on the floor. The women, on the other hand, were eager to begin the womaning process.

Connect to Give, Not Connect to Get
Your Inner Samurai's Perspective on Networking and Selling
Ch. 11

We were a small group — maybe 15 people — and all but two of us were Jewish. The other non-Jewish person was a practicing Zen Buddhist. She had a very gentle spirit and was contemplative, so her womaning was done in a very quiet manner. The other people in the room, more than half of them Jewish women over 40, were much more active in their womaning. Now, if you haven't been brought up in a Jewish home or had the unique experience of hanging around with lots of Jewish women, you might find this particular kind of womaning process a bit intrusive. For me, it had been a long time since I had spent a weekend with a group of Jewish mothers and grandmothers, so I was pleasantly warmed by the encounter.

The minute I walked through the door Saturday morning, all eyes were on me. Maybe this was because I was so obviously a Shiksa (a non-Jewish woman), although I doubt it. The Jewish women in the group were naturally curious. Knowing that they had only one weekend to connect and find out all they could about me, they set about doing so immediately. After two wonderfully helpful and kind men helped me get settled, the woman on my left started in immediately.

> "Oh, honey, that's a lovely color for you." She lightly fingered my linen shirt.
>
> "And such pretty hair," a woman on my right said. There was a round of nods and open murmurs of approval from the rest of the women in the group.
>
> "Glad you could join us and add your perspective," another added. "You're not Buddhist and not Jewish. You must be Catholic."

I smiled, not at all bothered by their interest. I was curious about them, too. But, why did they think I was Catholic? Oh, yeah. My light skin and blond hair. The only other non-Jewish person in the room was the Buddhist woman. She clearly looked Buddhist, with the soft warm-brown skin of Indian women and she was wearing a beautiful Sari. I bet they complimented her on how beautifully the green fabric showed off her dark brown eyes and skin.

As we were expertly guided to explore the parallels between the Jewish esoteric studies of the Zohar and the inner path teachings of the Tibetan Buddhist world of dzogchen ("the great perfection"), the women's interest in me increased. When I asked a particularly penetrating question of Rabbi Cooper about quantum physics, one woman on my left leaned across the woman next to her and whispered loudly to me, "Are you a scientist, dear?"

I shook my head no, with a warm smile on my face.

"Well, you sure seem to know a lot about physics," the woman said. And so it continued . . . womaning.

Now, some people might be put off by all these questions. I wasn't. In fact, I felt all tender and rosy inside whenever I was around these Jewish women. No matter where I was on the Omega Campus, if we saw one another, we would wave, beckon, and connect. We connected over lunch, after dinner, and at the Omega Café in the evening over vegan brownies. "They are so much better for you," they said, patting my arm.

We stood beside each other during T'ai Chi in the morning, sat beside each other in the Zen garden in the evening, and always stopped to chat on the way to or from the bathroom during breaks. I just loved these women.

They reminded me of my Momacita. How my Momacita loved people. All kinds of people. Old people, young people, people from all walks of life. It didn't matter to her if you were black, white, or purple. If you were Christian, Sufi, or Theravadan Buddhist. She just loved people. Momacita did womaning well. And while I may not have appreciated her womaning as a teenager and young adult, I did come to value it as I matured. Two years after her passing, I miss it even more. Having Jewish women womaning me that weekend felt so much like my Momacita, it touched my heart.

I think womaning is an art. We all have it, though some develop it more than others. Momacita was a master at it. In fact, when I read my part of the Eulogy at her Memorial Service in February 2005, I spoke about this amazing gift of hers that I knew every woman at the service would recognize.

> There wasn't a person that Roseann B. Reid did not befriend. I used to kid her that the only friend she had not met was someone she did not yet know, and of those she did not yet know, she was already considering them to be her best friend. Mom and I used to go to *Trader Jacks* on the weekend. As anyone who has also gone with her to this marvelous flea market can attest, it was near impossible to take five steps without her coming in contact with yet another friend she knew . . . or was just meeting. And once she met someone, she would find out their whole life story, sharing the details of her life along the way, connect them with someone she knew who went to school with so-and-so who

lived down the road about 25 years ago, and then invite them over to her house for a cup of tea and a look at the garden.

I Hate Being Sold to, But I Like to Buy

Recently, my guest on my *Accidental Pren-her: Stories of the Unexpected* podcast show was Pam Peyron, Educator and Director with USANA Health Sciences. I first met Pam in September of 2006 when she phoned in to a group call I was facilitating on prosperity. She also phoned in the next month, and afterward we struck up an Internet connection. Over the next nine months, we kept track of each other, supporting each other's successes, and following each other's progress.

Then, I received a postcard in the mail announcing her new combination website and blog start-up. I immediately went to www.ruralentrepreneurs.com and was intrigued. I really liked her variety, the way she was consciously going about building community, and how she was sharing her entrepreneurial journey with others. That's why I asked her to be a guest on my show. During the interview, one of the things she said was, "People buy us, and then they buy what we have to offer." When I thought about it, I knew she was right. Especially right for women.

Women like to *buy in* before they *buy*. Men do, too. Men, however, will more likely buy into *the value of the product* before they buy. Women are more likely to buy into *the seller*. This is a key difference between marketing to men and marketing to women.

Connect to Give, Not Connect to Get
Your Inner Samurai's Perspective on Networking and Selling
Ch. 11

The other day at Lowe's, I was pricing out sliding glass doors for the four-season room on the back of my home. One of the door panels had become damaged during a recent hailstorm when a limb broke and crashed into the window. When I arrived in the door department, the sales person was helping a couple with some questions. This gave me plenty of time to observe different buying styles in action.

The sales associate was doing a great job answering their questions. Together, he and the husband were talking about the energy efficiency of high-performance glazing. Was it better to go with dual glazing or double-paned glass with low emissivity coating? The husband ran his hands over the vinyl cladding around the outside of the door and asked about the practicality of top-mounted insect screens. There was a lot of verbal interaction as the husband sized up the product and relative value of the product in relation to the price listed.

The wife stood quietly nearby. She was not disinterested, mind you. She was just sizing up the product in a different way. She was watching the sales associate. She was deciding whether to buy into *him* and what he was saying. So, she asked another type of question: "What do you think about the sliding glass doors that have the curable vinyl cladding on the outside and the warmth of wood on the inside?" Note that she asked, "What do *you* think?" Asking a specific question about the product was just the vehicle for her to find out more about the sales associate's ideas, thoughts, and information. In short, about *him*.

When she spoke, she looked him straight in his eyes. While he referenced the sliding glass door by looking at it when he answered her, she barely gave the door a glance. She had already evaluated the door. Plus, she could tell from her husband's questions and responses that he was already considering the purchase. She wanted to know if she could trust the sales associate. Her body language and type of question was indicative of someone who is considering buying *into a person*. Pam's statement of "people buy us, and then they buy what we have to offer" rang true. This was so obvious in the buying styles of this husband and wife. The husband was considering the value of the product. The wife was considering the trustability of the sales person.

They also did my work for me. When the sales person asked if he could help me, I said, "No thanks. I just need a couple of prices so I can comparison shop." Then I turned to the couple and said, "Thank you! You guys were great!" They looked at each other, puzzled. They had no way of knowing that they'd just given me the perfect example of the difference in marketing to men and women.

BUILD THE RELATIONSHIP . . . AND THEY WILL COME

I know, I know, it's often overused, but it's true! From the Inner Samurai's perspective, the emphasis is on building relationships. What type of relationship? It could be called friendship. It could be called collegial. It could be called a business relationship. It could be called just about anything. However, the important aspect of the relationship is that it has to be a caring, quality relationship. No, not the co-dependent kind. I'm talking about a relationship where one person actually takes a genuine interest in who another person is. As my salesman friend Sam says: "It's about seeing others."

From the Inner Samurai's perspective, there are countless ways to position yourself for the natural alignment of connections to occur so that synergistic events will manifest. It's about putting yourself out there. It doesn't matter if you are out there on the Internet or out there at a networking convention. To the Inner Samurai, it really doesn't matter where you go or what type of events you attend, only that you are in alignment with these events and open to connecting with others.

The point is: Get out there. Do something. Take action. Move in some direction. Then let connections occur and synergetic events manifest.

Synchronistic Events, the Business Card of Choice

The business cards that we all carry around and pass out to others are of no great importance to your Inner Samurai. Synchronistic events, on the other hand, are. If you feel energetically aligned with asking someone for their business card or giving them yours, then do so. If you feel an inner, synchronistic pulse to ask them to dinner, arrange for another meeting time, or invite them out for a game of tennis, that's even better. That's the Inner Samurai business card of choice. You are receiving thousands of pulses a day from your Inner Samurai to take action. That amounts to a lot more contacts than you could ever hope to gather, process, and follow up on from a year's worth of networking events.

Synchronistic events. I'm sure you've had a number of these happen to you. I bet you'll know exactly what I mean when I tell you about my client Carrie. Carrie was at the point in her small business start-up when it was time for her to seek the advice of a small business attorney about what type of business structure would be best for her. We had already talked about the benefits and drawbacks to sole proprietorships, corporations, and partnerships. I am not an attorney, however. Also, I think it's a good idea for my clients to develop relationships with professionals who can guide their business from a legal standpoint. So, I suggested she find an attorney to help her.

For two months, Carrie resisted. Each week she would come to our coaching calls with everything done except making contact with a small business attorney. Finally, one week, the only assignment I gave her was to make contact. Pause. I could almost feel the color drain from her face across the phone line.

"Carrie? Are you okay?" I asked.

"Yeah." Then she changed her mind. "No, not really."

"Okay, tell me what's going on."

"I don't know any small business attorneys."

I was relieved to know that's all it was. "That's okay. Pull out your Yellow Pages and let's go through the list together."

At the end of our call, Carrie had narrowed her list to three promising small business attorneys that she said she would call.

At our next session, she reported that none of the people she talked with had given her good vibes and she wasn't any farther along in her search. In fact, in all but one case, she hadn't even asked the secretary to put her through to the attorney. Sensing there was something more going on here, I asked, "So, what do you think is really holding you back from contacting an attorney?"

> "I don't feel right about talking to a stranger about something so important to me."

Ah. I understood! "I don't like to do that, either."

> "It would be easier if I just knew someone, or knew of someone who knew someone."

"Well, I bet you do," I assured her.

Over the next two weeks, Carrie and I played a game I like to call, *Build the Relationship, and They Will Come.* I love playing this game with my clients and use it a lot in my own personal and business life.

> "Okay, Carrie, tell me what your perfect small business attorney relationship would look like."

> "Well," she began, "I'd like her to be knowledgeable, personable, take a genuine interest in my business, and base her fees on value rather than time."

Carrie and I had previously worked on her "money = value" mindset, so this was a good step forward. "Great! Now, are you open for your story to change?"

> "What story?" she asked, sounding perplexed.

> "That you will build a great relationship with this small business attorney after you find her."

219

Carrie was quick — she'd been working with me for a while now, so she smelled a reframing of her perspective coming on.

> "Yeah, you're right," she said. "I've got it backwards, don't I? I think that the relationship will come *after* I've found Ms. Perfect, not before."
>
> "Most people do," I smiled as I spoke so she could feel my warmth and support. "So, are you open for that story to change?"
>
> Yes!" she immediately responded. "Let's change that one right away. That story is history. I have a great relationship now and soon it will manifest."
>
> "There you go!"

Follow Your Inner Samurai's Lead

Because Carrie had reframed her story and shifted her perspective, over the next couple of days *seemingly* random events took place. First, she noticed more and more people talking about the law and lawyers. She began noticing what radio and TV attorney advertisements were saying. Then, one Sunday afternoon as she was walking back to her home from her run in the park, she noticed her neighbor, Mr. Thomas, working outside in his flower garden. He always had such lovely gardens, and she had been meaning to say so for some time. So she followed her Inner Samurai's pulse to tell him so — now.

Mr. Thomas was so appreciative of her compliments that they chatted a bit about the daylilies that were blooming. Then Carrie went back to her home. The next morning, as she stepped outside for her morning run, she discovered a potted daylily plant waiting for her on the porch. The card read: "Here's a registered *Tom Collins* daylily for you. I hybridized it and got to name it myself."

Carrie immediately went over to Mr. Thomas' house to thank him for his gift. That was when she found out that his passion and hobby was hybridizing daylilies. He'd been doing this for 30 years and even had a couple registered with the American Hemerocallis Society. Carrie was impressed!

Then she recognized her Inner Samurai pulse. Registered? Might that mean he had used an attorney to help him? "No, the registration process isn't all that legal, at least not at this level. I do know of someone, though, who is quite pleased with a local attorney he is using. I'd be glad to put you two in touch with each other." Within two days, Carrie, Mr. Thomas, and his friend Mr. Sawyer, met over lunch. By the end of meal, Carrie had the name of Mr. Sawyer's attorney.

At our next coaching session, Carrie was brimming with excitement. It felt so good for her to have made some movement in the direction of a small business attorney that her story bubbled out. I just kept smiling as her story unfolded — one synchronistic event after another.

"Now what," she asked?

"Follow up on every synchronistic event that comes along," I advised. "Check in with your Inner Samurai to know what action to take. Keep deepening your relationship with the perfect attorney. Build the relationship . . . and it will come."

Sure enough, after a couple more synchronistic occurrences, Ms. Perfect Attorney did come into being. She was everything Carrie had come to know. Because Carrie had already built a relationship with this lawyer in her mind's eye, sharing her small business start-up idea felt easy and safe.

BUILDING RELATIONSHIPS ONE PERSON AT A TIME

Relationships are formed one person at a time. To your Inner Samurai, how or where you meet someone is unimportant. It's the journey afterward that matters. Each relationship journey unfolds in its own unique and special way. And just like a snowflake, there are no two alike.

Test this out for yourself. Think about the last five people who have connected with you. Are you currently having the same kind of relationship with each person? Do you feel the same degree of closeness to them all? Are some relationships taking longer to develop? Was there one person you instantly hit it off with? I bet your relationships are like mine — unfolding in infinitely varied ways.

That's the beauty of relationships. They come, they go, they ebb, and they flow. Some people come into our lives with a quick burst of energy, burning bright and hot, while others simmer and take years to come to fruition. From your Inner Samurai's perspective, how and when they unfold is exactly the way they are meant to unfold.

Some relationships will be with you for life. These relationships will have stood the test of time and have deepened with age. Others will be shorter, coming together to complete a project or support to

Connect to Give, Not Connect to Get
Your Inner Samurai's Perspective on Networking and Selling

Ch. 11

each another through a particularly difficult time. Still other relationships continuously circle around and through the fabric of our lives, at times frequent and intense and at other times sporadic and distant. Yet, they are always there, connected. I have these kinds of relationships in my life and I know you do, too. These are the relationships where you can call the person after not talking for a long time and pick up just where you left off, as if you last talked just yesterday.

After the fabulously successful time Carrie had playing the *Build the Relationship, and They Will Come* game, she was ready to begin applying it to other areas of her business.

"Spend 80% of your time building relationships with people. Not networking. Not selling. Building," I began. "If you do it this way, your network will build, and your sales will come, quite naturally."

As 17th century English metaphysical poet John Donne wrote, "No man [or woman] is an island . . . ."[1] That quotation is no less true today than it was then. We don't thrive as well when we are isolated from others. We like to be in community with one another. We can't help but connect. Have you ever tried not running into someone? It's hard to do, isn't it? We're everywhere!

One final thing I told Carrie was to be a giver. And don't ever keep score of your giving. Don't keep track of who's done what, who owes whom a favor, or place a marker out there to be called in later. That's not The Way of your Inner Samurai. Give freely. Give to connect.

Have no worries, because people who establish strong connections and relationships with others never fail to create robust, thriving, successful businesses. People do business with those they know, like, and trust. Build relationships based on your Inner Samurai Guidance System. Your life will be rich beyond measure.

Notes from Your Inner Samurai

Relationships are all there is. Everything in the universe only exists because it is in relationship to everything else. Nothing exists in isolation. We have to stop pretending we are individuals and can go it alone.

— Margaret Wheatley

Cultivate relationships from the inside out. Base your relationships on giving to give, not giving to get. When pulsed to do so, give without reservation, regret, or expectation.

"Follow the Yellow Brick Road." Synchronistic events are your Inner Samurai's way of connecting and aligning you with all that is for your highest good and greatest well-being. Hey, it worked for Dorothy; it will work for you, too!

Rethink networking events from your Inner Samurai's perspective. They are just one of many countless places where you can go to allow synergistic events to manifest.

Practice the art of womaning. See everyone you meet as a relationship in the making. Ask questions. Give compliments. Listen and pay attention.

- Consider everyone you meet as an opportunity for you to give a gift or be given a gift.

- Remember the secret to Sam's sales success: "It's never about selling. It's about connecting to people and forming relationships with them. The same is true for networking. It's never about being seen, it's about seeing others."

- Remember the fluidity of relationships. Some will stay with you for life; others, not so long. Allow them to move in and out of your life with grace. Welcome them in love, let go of them in love, and cherish them for as long as they remain.

- Play the *Build the Relationship, and They Will Come* game often.

Chapter 12

HOME ALONE: THE DIFFERENCE BETWEEN ISOLATION AND SOLITUDE

Solitude vivifies; isolation kills.

— Joseph Roux

Ah, being a small business owner working from home has an immediate appeal, doesn't it?

What attracted you to starting a home-based Internet business? Was it the flexibility? Did you want to make sure you were home for your kids when they needed you? Maybe you were fed up with working for someone else. Perhaps it was just time — time to do the very thing you've always longed to do. Whatever the reason, one thing is for sure now: You are the big cheese, the go-to person. When it comes to your business, you have no one to rely on but yourself. The buck stops with you. Now, how does *that* feel?

Visions of hassle-free, dressed-down, low-interruption workdays rest easy on the mind. You get to do what you want to do, when you want to do it. There's no one else but you filling your daily schedule. There's no boss whose permission you need to leave work early so you can take your daughter to the doctor's office. There's no one you have to call to cover for you if you can't make it into work. You decide what you do and when you will do it. You chart your own course, set your own sail, and fly under your own colors. Can't you just feel the wind in your hair? The sun on your face? Feels great, doesn't it?

Being a small business owner means you get to decide . . . well, everything. You get to decide what your logo will look like. That's fun. You get to choose which product or service you develop first. It's nice not having someone else choose for you, isn't it? You get to decide when, you get to decide what, and you get to decide how much. Now, that's cool! You're in an enviable and powerful position. Best yet, you can do all this from the comfort of your home, within easy reach of the laundry room and coffee maker.

If you have a home-based Internet business, you can relocate at the drop of a hat. You can take your business with you wherever you go. "Have laptop, will travel." You can move your office out to your backyard deck on a beautiful day, you can take your projects to lunch at your favorite restaurant, and you can stay connected with your clients when you go skiing. All you need is a decent Internet and cell phone connection and you are good-to-go.

PARTY OF ONE

What's the catch?

Home Alone: The Difference Between Isolation and Solitude

Chances are, if you have a home-based Internet business, you are a party of one. While some people think this is the ideal situation, others consider this "freedom" to be the biggest drawback to their business. I know that was the case for me.

How about you? Was working from the comfort of your home just the ticket to removing all the outside distractions and interruptions that plagued your traditional work life? Or did you find it difficult to make the change from working with lots of people around you to working at home, alone, most of the day?

I'm an extrovert. I get my creative spark from stimulating interaction with the outside world. Are you are an extrovert, too? If so, I bet you can appreciate it when I say, with all the dramatic flare I can muster, that being isolated does me in! Before I became a home-based Internet business owner, my alone time needs had always been met by being *away* from work. With work and home in the same place, I had too much alone time on my hands. Working from home had become synonymous with working in isolation, and I knew I didn't like that.

Solitude is the state of being solitary or secluded.[1] I've certainly had a lot of experience with that over the years, and I bet you have, too. In fact, like me, I expect you enjoy being a party of one, every now and then. Maybe you actually seek out times to be on your own. I know I do. Whether it's early in the morning before the world awakens, or late at night when I shut my door to write in my journal, I highly value these alone times. As Omar Khayyam so eloquently put it, "The thoughtful soul to solitude retires."[2]

Though I often complained about students bombarding my office, the number of committees I served on, and colleagues who would just pop by for a chat, the truth was, I liked it. I liked my day being filled with thought-provoking conversations.

Ever listen to what young people are talking about these days? They have such wonderful thoughts and ideas! When I was in my office, I would often leave the door open. Within a short time, I would have a group of students hanging around sharing what was on their minds. Sometimes we laughed uproariously. Other times, our foreheads would furrow deep in concentrated thought. I found it fascinating to hear what my students were thinking about and always honored that they would share their thoughts with me. Afterward, I went home for some alone time, some down time. I liked this separation of stimulation and solitude.

That's the way it had been most of my adult working life. Work had one purpose and home had another. I liked that arrangement. Better said, I had become used to that arrangement — I knew no other. And it wasn't something I enjoyed just on a daily basis. On a larger scale, I looked forward to the start of each semester, and I also looked forward to semesters being over. I flourished, grew, and benefited from the stimulating 16-week semester when I knew I would be interacting and making music with my choirs. And I looked forward, with equal measure, to the longer periods off between semesters. I liked them both.

No More Separation of Stimulation and Solitude

Then came my new reality: Home and work were now sharing the same space. I was no longer getting my "stimulation fix" from a busy workplace, colleagues, and students. Now I was spending too much time alone. Isolation became a real issue for me. I was like a mother who spends her day relating only to little children, counting the hours until her husband comes home after work, just so she can talk about something other than Barney. I felt isolated and set apart from other people. In short, I was lonely.

So, I did the first thing that any sane woman would do. I called my girlfriends! The great thing about having lived and worked in so many places over the years was that I had friends in many places. I had friends on the west coast, the east coast, and in between. I had friends in Canada, Brazil, Costa Rica, England, Europe, and Greece. I had friends in Israel, Australia, Malaysia, Japan, and China. For the first time in my life, I could exclaim, "Thank heaven for time zones!"

Time zones were my salvation. I could call my friend Rhiannon in Wales first thing in the morning, my friend Sally in Oregon later in the afternoon, and my friend Allison in Australia at the end of the day. I became a master at time zone calculations. Who needs an atomic clock? Let's see . . . Sydney is GMT + 10. That means it's 5:49 a.m. there. Hmm, perhaps I should wait a couple of hours before I call Allison. But, wait! I can fit in my call to Helga in Munich first.

The mere fact that I was now thinking in Greenwich Mean Time, plus or minus, should have been a tip off. Instead of thinking that my friend Marla, living in California, was three hours behind me, as most people do, I was now in the GMT - 8 mode. You know how some people talk when they operate on 24-hour clock time? "What time is dinner tonight, dear?" "1900 hours. Don't be late." I would be thinking, I wonder if Eneken is available to talk? She's in Estonia. Yep, that would be GMT + 2.

There was one little problem with all this calling around the globe: money. Now, you know from my chapter on money that it's never about money; it's about value. After I had increased my domestic rate plan to include all the countries I was calling, plus Canada, I began using online phone cards. Those cards are great! Mostly. It took me a while to find the best one — I had all my international friends to help me with that. Then, it was just a matter of buying them in bulk, preferably on sale (value, folks, value). I also had to remember which card I was using, when I was using it, and whom and where I was calling. I soon realized the calling plan and calling cards were costing me a small fortune each month. When I considered the hassle factor, time spent searching for the best deal, dropped or missed calls, and the percentage of time people were actually home when I called, the value wasn't in line with the cost.

So, I switched to emailing.

Regardless, I was still not dealing with the problem — just coping with it.

READING YOUR INNER SAMURAI: YOUR INNER KNOWER

When you become a home-based, Internet business owner for the first time, one of the things that will quickly become apparent is the value of surrounding yourself with people who can support and guide you along your entrepreneurial journey. There are so many possibilities for support and guidance; I am sure you will not have any problem finding what you need. Some people rely on their family and friends. Others hire a coach or consultant. Many people take online classes. Others prefer to learn within a classroom. Most people buy books. A number of people travel for training, to attend seminars, and go to conferences. It's not so important what you do. It's only important that you balance your need for outside stimulation and interaction with your need for solitude.

Each of us is different, and our needs also fluctuate. The key is to become aware of what you need when. How do you do that? By getting really good at reading your Inner Samurai. Something frequently overlooked: there is a fine line between stimulation and frenetic activity, between solitude and isolation. The voice inside your head cannot distinguish the difference. However, your inner knower, your Inner Samurai, can. The way to know the difference is by checking in . . . often.

When you do, stimulation will feel inspirational, motivational, encouraging, and activating. Frenetic activity will feel frantic, chaotic, and feverish. When you are experiencing stimulation, you will feel your Inner Samurai harmoniously aligned with continued interaction. You will be getting an *all systems go* pulse from within — an internal green light, a *yes!*

If you are experiencing frenetic activity, you will be getting just the opposite from your Inner Samurai. You will feel discomfort and disease. You will feel scattered, as if you are going in a thousand directions and doing a million different things without getting much accomplished. If you check in with your Inner Samurai during this time, you will clearly feel a *no,* and be pulsed to move in the opposite direction. Continuing with frenetic activity will just make things more stressful. Soon anxiety will set in. This is your Inner Samurai's way of saying, "This is not in your best interest or for your greatest well-being."

Isolation will leave you feeling lonely and separated. Many people associate isolation with depression. Others experience it as remoteness. Still others say they feel secluded. My client Rita compared isolation with getting on an elevator that is going down without any stops. Actually, isolation and solitude are two different elevators. As Rita observed, isolation goes downward. The other elevator, solitude, goes inward. Isolation takes us away from our Inner Samurai. Solitude connects us to her.

When you choose to go inward to commune with your Inner Samurai, you experience inner focus. Work accomplished from this inner focusing place will be powerful, compelling, and moving. It will feel as if you have tapped into a refreshing reservoir of knowledge, an inner well of wisdom. What flows from this place is deeply inspirational.

Home Alone: The Difference Between Isolation and Solitude — Ch. 12

Here's something important to remember: We can have either an inward or an outward experience and still be aligned with our Inner Samurai. Solitude is the inward expression of that alignment. Stimulation is its outer expression. Isolation and frenetic activity, on the other hand, mean that we are not currently aligned with our Inner Samurai or moving in a direction she would sanction. Rita describes this Inner Samurai sanctioned direction as being "golden." Indeed, when you are moving in this powerful way, everything you touch and everything you do will feel like gold.

Pay attention to which kind of signals your Inner Samurai is pulsing to you. Does your body feel constricted or relaxed?

Constricted — Disconnected
Relaxed — Connected

Do you feel in the flow or are you pushing for outcome?

Flow — Connected
Pushing — Disconnected

Remember, too, that your Inner Samurai communicates to you in very clear language. When you take the time to go inward and check in, you will clearly feel *yes* and you will clearly feel *no*.

You will know the difference between your Inner Samurai and the voice inside your head by the type of response you get. If you check in and you get a lot of chatter, explanation, and reasoning, that is the voice inside your head. Learn to recognize and ignore it. If you check in and feel a one word pulse, pay attention. That is your Inner Samurai.

COMMUNITY: THE LIFE BLOOD OF HOME-BASED INTERNET BUSINESS OWNERS

If you are an Accidental Pren-her newly experiencing life outside of a traditional work environment, then you may be missing some very important things. Perhaps it's the group of people that you had grown used to having lunch with each day or the political repartee around the water cooler. Maybe it's Happy Hour after work on Friday, or someone to car pool with in the morning. Whatever it is, chances are you are missing some social interaction or sense of community that you had come to know and may have taken for granted.

For Rita, she wasn't really into socializing at work. Imagine her surprise when she discovered that, once she started her own business, the thing she missed the most was the built-in social interaction that her traditional work place afforded her.

By her own definition, Rita is a "closet introvert." She is shy by nature and not prone to go out and make friends on her own. Yet soon after she became an Accidental Pren-her, she began languishing from lack of social contact. This astounded her, because she had always thought of herself as someone who didn't like to be around people. She hadn't realized how much working with groups of people around her had actually filled her innate human need for social interaction — her need to connect.

At her former job, Rita was often frustrated because she was never able to be alone with her thoughts. She was unprepared, though, for having all the time in the world to be alone with her thoughts. At first, having plenty of time appealed to her, immensely. Rita reveled in extended periods of uninterrupted concentration. Her levels of creativity soared. Then, when she came up for air, she wanted someone to talk to. But there was no friend down the hall whose office door she could fling open, no water cooler to congregate around for a chat. Gone was the undeniable camaraderie that she had developed with her colleagues. Loneliness and depression began to creep in. Rita contemplated returning to the daily grind of an office job, just so she would have a social network.

THE AH-HA SISTERHOOD

I experienced this, too. That's why I was only too happy to join the Ah-Ha Sisterhood. The Ah-Ha Sisterhood was the brainchild of my dear friend, Lacy. Lacy is, by nature, someone who just has a knack for connecting people. Lacy had become a solo preneur two years before I did. So, from my perspective, she was an experienced solo preneur. She had her act together, knew what she was doing, and offered a tremendous wealth of support and experience. The trouble was, she lived 1,000 miles away.

As the way of all things great, Lacy was friends with two other people who were also in various stages of Accidental Pren-hership. Terry had quit her job a year after Lacy did and was just deciding what she wanted to do with her life. Jodi knew she would be leaving her corporate job in about nine months and was preparing for that transition. Then there was me who had just recently resigned from academia. All three of us were bombarding Lacy, asking for information, advice, and support.

One day, Lacy had the brilliant idea of getting us all together at her house to attend a Small Business start-up workshop being put on by Coach U.[3] So we all drove or flew in to stay with her and attend the workshop together. It was so much fun! We sat together at the workshop, passing ideas back and forth and brainstorming possibilities. Most of all, we laughed, laughed, and laughed. We ate together, slept in the same house, and talked late into the night. At the end of our time together, we had formed the Ah-Ha Sisterhood.

Partly inspired by the movie, *Divine Secrets of the Ya Ya Sisterhood*, and partly by the "ah-ha moments" that each of us was having in the start-up process, the name stuck. Though we lived in different states, we knew we had something special going on and vowed to find some way to continue our group. Enter the beauty of teleconferencing. Armed with an access number and bridge line, the Ah-Ha Sisterhood met to talk — first, each month, then biweekly, then every week. Together we inspired, supported, brainstormed, and problem-solved for each other. Sometimes we met individually. Usually, though, we preferred to meet together.

In addition to the Ah-Ha Sisterhood, I actively sought out two other people living near me who were also starting up businesses. Paul, Tom, and I met for dinner on Wednesday nights almost every week for a year. We kept our meeting time short. We gave each other just one hour from the time we placed our orders to discuss, bemoan, and problem solve anything related to business. Knowing that

Home Alone: The Difference Between Isolation and Solitude — Ch. 12

all we had was 60 minutes made our time together focused and results-oriented. Each of us came with questions and left with answers.

Although the Ah-Ha Sisterhood no longer meets, and Paul, Tom, and I have evolved to meeting on a quarterly basis for 90-minute dinners, the special bond of friendship that developed because of our collective need for community still stands. Neither time nor space could ever negate what we all went through together. Moreover, we continue to be there for each other, whenever the need arises.

Without Lacy, Terry, Jodi, Tom, and Paul, it is likely I would have made a very common mistake among new small business owners: I would have bailed too soon, before I had really given this solo preneur thing a fair shot. Establishing these business-related social communities saved me from myself. I cannot stress enough how valuable it is to gather together a supportive group of people who know what you are going through and are willing to spend time with you processing and brainstorming. Your Inner Samurai knows this, too, and will guide you to exactly the right people at the right time.

FIVE CARD FLUSH, ACE HIGH

Since she missed social interaction and connecting with others, I urged Rita to get out of the house and join some like-minded people for an activity or sport. The emphasis was on joining a group. If you're like Rita, almost any kind of group will do: a tennis league, garden club, travel group, or gourmet dinner club. Think of the things you enjoy doing, then look for opportunities in your area. Take care not to choose a "party of one" group. Anything described as a party of one, technically, isn't a group. And, by the way, meditation groups don't count. You need to be part of a group that talks. In Rita's case, I also suggested that she find a group she could join during the week, when other home-based people would be available to gather.

I joined a poker group two years after I started my business. Every Wednesday afternoon at 3:00 p.m., I hop on my bike (weather permitting) and pedal 20 minutes up the mountain to join a group of home-based small business owners for a game of poker at our local country club. We all lead busy lives, so the group members come and go. The only requirement is that, when you do attend, you come to play. Sometimes we play for money. Other times we play for business cards. Sometimes we play for a massage, a golf package or some other goodie that one of our members has drummed up.

In addition to playing poker, we also talk business. In between bluffing, posturing, and throwing our cards down with an "I-don't-have-squat" flourish, we talk business. When we play round robin games, we get the added benefit of taking whatever question we have to several other tables, eliciting a wealth of ideas and opinions. Oftentimes you will hear, "Hey, I want to play at Paula's table because I want to pick her brain." By now we've all become familiar with each other's specialty and area of expertise. That makes it easy to pass along a referral.

After one hour together, we leave as quickly as we came. The poker tables are emptied, the chips neatly stacked. Some of us get on bikes and race each other downhill, others get in a few laps at the pool or work out before going home, and still others toot and wave as they leave the parking lot. When we see each other around, there is a cheery, warm feeling inside. Community is the life-blood to home-based, small online business owners.

GET HIP TO BLOGGING

Do you blog? Have a blog? Know how to post on a blog? Do you think this topic doesn't apply to you and want to skip this part of the chapter? I know, I know. There was a time, not so long ago, when I would have skipped right over this section, too, with a dismissive, "Whatever." Just hang on a minute. News flash: blogging is for business owners, too. The total number of business blogs is growing. More than that, business blogs are some of the most interesting and powerful opportunities for communication, education, reporting, publishing, and grassroots innovation that have appeared in recent years. Get over the 'blog' label. Think of it as conversation . . . with peers, clients, prospects, and more.

If you are a home-based, Internet business owner, having a business blog relating to your products and services is an invaluable tool. When I told this to Rita, she just rolled her eyes.

"Susan, seriously, can you see me, at my age, blogging?" (Rita is 45).

"Yes. Absolutely!"

"Well, what would I blog about?"

"What do you want to blog about?"

"Nothing. I see no reason to blog."

Ah... and herein lies the biggest challenge to anyone who becomes an Accidental Pren-her in her 40s. You're simply not used to blogging. You don't yet see the value in blogging, and, frankly, aren't sure you want to. That was the case for Rita, too. She could see the importance of having a mission statement, determining her niche market, developing her products, and putting together a business plan. She knew how significant having a website, web presence, and marketing strategy was to her business. But blogging? Blogging was another story.

If you have never blogged or owned a blog, it's possible you feel the same way — and you don't stand alone. Just look around your group of friends and count how many people blog or have a blog.

> When I asked Rita that question she said, "You're the only one I know."
>
> "And how many times have you visited my blog?" I asked.
>
> "None."

Well, okay, besides the fact that she didn't earn any brownie points for that answer, that is a pretty common response for women in their 40s and 50s.

Just as those in their 60s and 70s were left out of the computer generation, those in their 40s and 50s have been left out of blogging. However, many people in the 60s and 70s have discovered that computers are cool. I remember bugging my parents for a year to subscribe to an Internet provider so they could get online. They had already been long-time computer users, but thought the whole Internet thing was just not for them.

So, for Christmas one year I bought them a year's subscription to AOL. They didn't seem all that jazzed about the gift. They smiled as if to say, "We saw this coming." I installed it and set everything up. Then I walked each of them through their first online session. I went to bed at 10:00 p.m. in the library guest bedroom. At 3:00 a.m., when I got up to go to the bathroom, their desk lights were still on. "Leon," Momacita animatedly called out to Dad, "I just googled *pizzeles* and look at all these recipes I found!" I smiled. They were hooked. A whole new world had just opened for them. A world they never knew existed. Within weeks, they were sending me links to check out. What a couple of pros!

That's how it is with blogging.

> "Let's get started blogging," I said to Rita one day during a coaching session.
>
> "Okay," she reluctantly agreed. Within 30 minutes Rita was up and running. "Wow, that was fast and easy," she said. "Now what?"
>
> "What's the #1 thing you want people to know about your business?"
>
> "I want people to know about my services." (Rita is a transition consultant specializing in working with people who are moving out of a corporate career into a green/environmental career.)
>
> "Perfect. Now, let's brainstorm topics that your niche market would be interested in."

Within a short period, Rita had come up with five great ideas: how to go green, green job boards, green in the news, managing green transitions, and green carrot-and-stick.

"Excellent! Now let's set up an editorial blogging calendar.[4] Let's make Monday your *how to go green* day; Tuesday, your *green job boards* day; Wednesday, your *green in the news* day; Thursday, your *managing green transitions* day; and Friday, your fun *green carrot-and-stick* day."

These became Rita's five main categories. I encouraged her to blog every weekday on these topics for six months straight. Once she saw it broken down into manageable parts with definable topics, Rita proclaimed, "I can do that!"

Nine months later, Rita is still enthusiastically blogging. She enjoys the community she has created, the other people she has met through her blogging efforts, and the connections she has made. She easily bridged the blogging gap and is now unreservedly recommending blogging to her friends and business associates. Rita's blog has driven traffic to her website and is one of the top ways people in her niche market find her. Her blog has become a cozy place to come and hang out. It's a great place for potential clients to informally come and get to know Rita before making direct contact.

As my realtor friend Murray says, "Open house is to house sales as blogging is to web sales." People come to open houses to see a house, gather information, and check out the realtor. Blogs serve the very same purpose for the small business owner. In addition, they are a great way to make home alone fun!

NOTES FROM YOUR INNER SAMURAI

Solitude has its own very strange beauty to it.

— Liv Tyler

- Know how much solitude you like and how much social stimulation you need. Then give yourself permission to have both.

- If you are feeling isolated, reach out to trusted friends, family, and professionals for help and support.

- Get accustomed to the voice of your Inner Samurai. Become attuned to her inner pulse.

- Make no excuse. Listen for the *yes* or *no* of your Inner Samurai. Then, have courage to follow her inner knowing with conviction and purpose.

- Reach out to others who have been there, done that. There is no need to reinvent the wheel when there are so many wonderfully helpful people ready to share what they know.

- Think of blogging as just another way to make friends and form new relationships.

- Bridge the blogging gap. You will be overjoyed with the new world that awaits you.

Connecting and sharing is an instinctive human need. Tap into your Inner Samurai for the perfect people, places, and ways to do just that.

Chapter 13

SCHEDULING CHAOS

A schedule defends from chaos and whim. It is a net for catching days. It is a scaffolding on which a worker can stand and labor with both hands at sections of time.

— Annie Dillard

Have you ever considered what your day would be like if you had absolutely no schedule? Nothing and no one telling you where to go, what to do, or when to do it? If you could wake up when you wanted to, go to bed when you wanted to, and do anything and everything in-between, what would that be like?

I certainly had no idea. I had never experienced such a time. Even on days off or vacations, I always had some sort of plan running around inside my head. Even if it was a vague plan — Sometime this afternoon I think I will go shopping — and even if I never got around to fulfilling my intention, it was still a plan.

When I resigned from my job and became an Accidental Pren-her, things changed.

For a while, I persisted in having a loose running game plan for my day. It's Tuesday. OK, I will call to see if I can get my car serviced on Friday. It's Wednesday. That means Tai Chi class at 10:00 a.m. Nothing too taxing, nothing too stressful. My schedule was far more flexible than what it had been while working at the university. Even with no schedule imposed upon me, however, I remember noticing that I was still planning my day as if I had a mandatory schedule. I was a schedule junkie.

What's a Nice Girl Like You Doing Without a Plan?

That's one of the first questions I asked my new client, Victoria. Victoria had recently been downsized from a company she had been with for over 20 years. Although she had been given six month's notice, it was still a devastating experience for her. Being the smart Accidental Pren-her that she is, Victoria negotiated a generous nine-month severance package that included full benefits, salary, and work with an executive coach who specialized in corporate transitions.

Victoria chose to work with me because of my forte working with creative entrepreneurial women who come from a corporate setting. Once Victoria moved beyond the initial shock of not going to work every day, she saw her Accidental Pren-her situation as a chance to see if she could make a living from something she loved. "I'm a closet milliner," she confessed. "I'm good at it, and I love it. I've not gone in this direction full-time because I'm not sure if I can bring in the money I want just through designing and selling women's hats."

Victoria's interest in hats went far back into her childhood. When she was eight years old, her grandmother taught her how to sew. That's when her love affair with fabric began.

She was enchanted with her mother's hats. When she was tall enough to reach the top shelf of her mother's walk-in closet, Victoria would stand on tiptoe and with her fingertips she would coax a stack of beautifully bound and braided hatboxes down from the shelf. Then, she would carefully remove the protective tissue paper from each hat and examine them, fascinated with their construction and design. For hours she filled sketchbook after sketchbook of her mother's hats from every conceivable angle. She'd take copious notes about what fabrics were used and how they were shaped. Because her mother had fantastic taste, Victoria developed a sophisticated palate for couture hats.

Starting in eighth grade, Victoria began designing custom-made, individually handcrafted hats for her mom and her mom's friends. She had a hat idea for every season and reason. Taking inspiration for her hats from whatever occasion she was designing for, whether it was a wedding, holiday, or the Kentucky Derby, Victoria became known around town as, "The Hat Girl."

Much to everyone's surprise, after high school Victoria eschewed going on to a fashion design school, preferring instead to get a sensible degree in industrial engineering from the University of Oregon. She did well in school and was hired on directly after graduation to work at Nike®. Her sensible corporate career had begun.

However, Victoria hadn't given up hats completely. Once she got settled at Nike, she converted one of her apartment bedrooms into a design studio so she could make hats from home. Although she made practical hats, what she really liked designing were elegant haute couture hats. That's when she discovered world famous milliner, Jeanne Bjorn. Bjorn was teaching millinery classes from her studio in Portland, Oregon. That was so close to where Victoria lived that she soon became a regular class member. So, by day, she was Vicky, industrial engineer, and by night, she was Victoria, haute couture designer. She thrived living this double life.

All that ended in 2005. Her job was outsourced. Victoria didn't know what she was going to do. She was scared to death of launching her designs and pursuing her passion on a full-time basis. Therefore, she avoided doing anything about it for three more months. She didn't look for work. She didn't sell any hats. She put all her orders on hold. She was too paralyzed to move forward with her hat business. She had liked living a double life. Now she no longer had the security and safety of her sensible day job. Could she bring her haute couture evening and weekend job into the light? Victoria just didn't know. Most of all, she feared that, if she "came out," she would end up hating millinery — something she never wanted to happen.

Living off her severance package, she met friends for lunch, took her mother shopping, worked out, and didn't accept any new hat orders. Unfettered by a corporate schedule for the first time in 20 years, Victoria was having the time of her life. Victoria began her day at 6:00 a.m. or noon, whichever suited her at the time. She played golf during the week, read for hours at a time in the middle of the day, and lost all track of whether it was a weekday or the weekend. Her day lasted as long as it lasted and ended when she said it did. No one and nothing was on her schedule. That's just the way she liked it.

To the casual observer, it might look as if Victoria had it made. Upon closer examination, she was dust in the wind. Victoria lacked structure, focus, and purpose, and this was driving her crazy! It was driving her millinery customers crazy, too. In fact, that was part of the reason she came to me: She didn't know what to do with her customers!

Niche Ready and Customers Banging Down Doors

What an amazing position to be in. Victoria had customers. She had a client list. She even had a back order list. She had been making hats for 30 years. People had come to know her, trust her, buy from her, order from her, and recommend her to others. Now . . . where in the world was Victoria? Victoria was MIA. She was working on her golf swing, catching up on her novels, and screening her phone calls.

Most clients who come to me don't have an established niche. They don't have products. They don't know if they have a viable, sustainable, financially profitable product. Victoria did! She was in an enviable position. Most of my other clients would have given their eyeteeth to be where she was.

Victoria saw it differently. "Everyone wants me to open up a store, to go into business for myself. Everyone is telling me that this is a chance of a lifetime and that I should take advantage of my windfall."

"What do you think?" I asked her.

"I think not," she said.

"Okay, then, how come we're talking?"

"Because I heard you were good."

I was puzzled by that response. "Good at what?"

"Good at getting people lined up with their passion."

"Ah," I said, "Now we're talking. Is that what you want?"

"I don't know. I guess."

"You guess?"

"Okay, yes," she replied, as if I had twisted her arm.

I laughed. "Hey, Victoria?"

"Yeah?"

"Newsflash: I'm only as good as my clients allow me to be. I'm only as good as they want to be themselves. How good do you want to be?"

Silence.

More silence. (As you might remember, I'm good with silence.)

"Truth?" she asked.

"Truth," I insisted.

I could hear her take a deep breath and hold it. "I want to be really, *really* good!"

"So," I asked her with a smile in my voice, "What's a nice girl like you doing without a plan?"

SETTING YOUR ENERGETIC SCHEDULE

Over the next couple of months together, Victoria and I examined each perceived fear she had around opening her own business. The more we examined, the more she softened around the edges. Little by little, Victoria began answering the phone, talking with her customers, and getting back into her creative flow. It was a beautiful experience to be a part of. I felt as if I were watching a lotus flower opening.

Victoria was feeling better, she was less anxious and more excited about her future, and had now brought her nighttime hobby into the light of day. Victoria's schedule was still erratic, though.

> One day she blurted out, "My schedule is getting in the way of me!"
>
> "Oh, how so?" I inquired.
>
> "I'm so messed up with my schedule. I'm all over the place," she lamented.
>
> "Victoria, if you could schedule your day any way you wanted it, what would it look like?"
>
> "Exactly how it is," she countered, defensively.
>
> "Really? How's that working out for you?"
>
> "Not so great," she conceded. "I mean, I like doing all the things I'm doing. I don't want that to stop. But something is off. I just don't know what."
>
> "So, is there anything you would like to change about your day?"
>
> She thought for a moment. "Well, yes, there is. While I really enjoy all the flexibility and spontaneity I have during the day, I'm

exhausting myself. I haven't gotten myself into a schedule that suits me. I don't eat at regular intervals, my sleep cycle is off, and I feel lackluster."

I hear this a lot from people used to working in a corporate environment. It's a combination of being home alone, sometimes for the first time (as I talked about in the previous chapter), and being accustomed to someone else setting your schedule for you. Working from home is often a jarring experience for those of us who make that transition. I know it was for me. Was it the same for you? Did you have a hard time getting into the swing of things? Was it hard finding your groove? Did you even know what your groove was? I know I didn't, until I encountered the energetic calendar.

Scheduling from the Inside Out

What's an energetic calendar? It's your Inner Samurai's answer to scheduling. Created from the inside out, an energetic calendar is based on your energetic resonance and alignment during the day. My business coach, BZ Riger of www.InnerGametoWealth.com, introduced this concept to me. It made all the difference in the world.

Like Victoria, I had come from a corporate environment — corporate academia. I was used to a corporate schedule. I was told when my choirs would rehearse, when my classes would meet, and how much time a week I should set aside for office hours. Then I had the flexibility to schedule anything else the way I wanted it. This was no different from any other job I had. From my high school job teaching swim classes at the YMCA, to working as a

Minister of Music and Youth in churches, to working as a therapist, to conducting, someone else had always set my work schedule.

This was the same for Victoria. When I introduced her to the idea of an energetic calendar, she had no idea what I was talking about.

"It's the calendar of your Inner Samurai," I explained. "The purpose of an energetic calendar is to become aware of what hours of the day you feel most pulsed to do things. What days resonate with what activities, and what parts of the day feel best for you to do what." If you've never thought about your time in this way before, this concept could be blowing your mind. I know it was that way with me when BZ first introduced it to me.

At first, Victoria had no idea how she energetically resonated with each day. Most people don't. In fact, when my business coach first introduced me to this concept, I had a hard time figuring out what she meant. So, I started Victoria out gently.

> "For one whole week, keep track of the things you feel drawn to do during the day and night. Make a note of the times during the week that you like doing them."

"Okay," she said, a little hesitantly.

The next week, Victoria had a list of 47 things she did during the week.

> "Uh, no," I began, "I didn't want your to-do list for the week. I wanted your like-to-do list." Remembering how I had struggled with this assignment myself, I guided her by asking, "What on this list do you like to do? What lights you up?"

"I like to walk my dogs in the morning, do Pilates or something else physical in the afternoon, work on my hats in the late morning and early evening, and get out of the house around noon."

This was a good start. "Anything else?"

"You know, I haven't done much of it lately, but I like to sketch."

"Sketch. Okay. When do you sense is your best time to sketch?"

"Seriously? Do you really want my honest answer?"

"Yes!"

"I like to sketch in the quiet of the morning, before anyone else is up."

"When would that be?" I nudged.

"3:00 a.m.," she admitted, as if it were a deep dark secret she had been holding for a long time.

And so we began. The next week Victoria came back with a calendar that had 24 hours in a day. She had expanded her energetic calendar from 12 to 24 hours. She had also decided to start her workweek on Tuesday, building into her schedule a day off just to be. When I asked her about this, she said,

"Monday is just not that great of a day for me. Since this calendar is about me and what resonates with me, then purposefully not having anything to do on Monday works for me."

Perfect. This was exactly what I wanted to see and hear from Victoria. I wanted her to make energetic choices based on what worked for her, not on how she had done things in the past. Over the next couple of weeks, Victoria tuned in more and more to her Inner Samurai. She tuned in to another way of being during her day, week, and month. When doing so, she found that she was, naturally, a very early riser. Now that she no longer had to get up in the morning to be at work by a certain time, Victoria was surprised that she actually felt pulsed to get up even earlier.

> "This is strange," she confided one day, "I used to complain about having to get up early when I worked for Nike®. I always felt tired. Now, I awaken easily at 3:00 a.m., pad downstairs for a hot cup of herbal tea, crawl back under the covers, open up my sketchbook and draw."

After a month of tuning into her Inner Samurai Scheduler, Victoria had a weekly energetic calendar that was beautifully aligned with her particular style and way of doing things. Additionally, Victoria stopped complaining. She was getting plenty of sleep, was eating well, doing all the things she wanted to do during the day, and getting loads of millinery work done.

Nearly nine months after leaving Nike®, with her severance package getting ready to expire, Victoria had come full circle. With her ready-made client list and customer orders, she was now a thriving small business owner. Victoria had done what all of us dream of doing. She had turned her passion into a profitable product. She was working full-time at something she was deeply interested in doing — something that tapped into her creative juices and kept them overflowing with ideas. She was excited to get up in the morning and begin her day, and she was pleasantly content at the end.

Victoria had a clear mind. She had focus, structure, and purpose. Victoria had come into her own. Pablo Picasso describes it perfectly: "My mother said to me, 'If you become a soldier, you'll be a general; if you become a monk, you'll end up as the Pope.' Instead, I became a painter and wound up as Picasso." Victoria had discovered her Picasso.

> "My engine purrs," she said one day. "I feel like that Silver Porsche Cayman I've had my eye on."

I chuckled with her, tickled by how she was now expressing herself.

WHAT A DIFFERENCE THE RIGHT SCHEDULE CAN MAKE

The Annie Dillard quotation at the beginning of this chapter sums up, very well, what a difference the right schedule can make in your life: "A schedule defends from chaos and whim. It is a net for catching days. It is a scaffolding on which a worker can stand and labor with both hands at sections of time." Whether it is an Inner Samurai energetic calendar or a more traditional schedule, having a schedule that is accommodating, flexible, and created from within, is invaluable.

A schedule defends from chaos and whim. My friend Carrie calls her schedule her container. It's the container of her day. She likes the idea of working from within a container. It makes her feel safe and, at the same time, opens her up to be creative.

Scheduling Chaos — Ch. 13

It is a net for catching days. Whenever I contemplate Dillard's quotation, I smile every time I schedule a client call, an evening out, or time alone. I see in my mind's eye a big, huge butterfly net gently enfolding the time, so I can explore and delight in each day.

It is a scaffolding on which a worker can stand and labor with both hands at sections of time. This is Victoria's favorite part of the quotation.

> "I can actually feel that scaffolding beneath my feet; whereas, before, scheduling felt like a noose around my neck. It allows me to be very focused and intentional about everything I do. It is the underpinning of my day."

NOTES FROM YOUR INNER SAMURAI

*Get rid of things, or you'll spend
your whole life tidying up.*

— Marguerite Duras

Take note of the things you were wildly interested in as a child and teen. Are you still interested in them? Are these the hobbies you are still finding time to do? If so, consider turning them into a profitable business.

Every perceived tragedy is a gift in disguise. Being downsized, outsourced, or fired from your corporate job might just well be the very thing you need to propel you into the next great manifestation of your life.

You are in an enviable position — all the time. Just because you don't know it, doesn't mean it isn't so. Look around. Take stock. What do you have going for you that no one else does? Could be the beginning of a unique product or service.

Consider creating your own personalized schedule. One made just for you from the inside out. Custom designed by the Master Scheduler herself — your Inner Samurai.

Scheduling Chaos — Ch. 13

- Make as many energetically aligned choices about what to do each day as possible. Your body will thank you.

- Allow your energetic schedule to turn your chaos into clarity and your untidiness into a beautiful butterfly net for catching opportunities.

Chapter 14

THE SECRET TO YOUR BUSINESS SUCCESS

*Keep walking, though there's no place to get to.
Don't try to see through the distances. That's
not for human beings. Move within, but don't
move the way fear makes you move.*

— Rumi

You've probably heard the phrase, "Mi casa, su casa" ("My house is your house"). It's such a great phrase, isn't it? It's at once warm and comforting. It brings up images of genially welcomed visitors, familiar and known, roaming about as if they have lived in your home all their lives.

We all have our special ways of welcoming people into our home and setting the stage for what we want them to experience. What are some of yours? Some people put fresh flowers on the bedside table. Others cook a special meal. Still others greet their visitors with warm smiles, big hugs, and a ready glass of wine. No matter what the gesture, it means the same thing: Make yourself at home. Feel free to help yourself to whatever you want. Treat my home as if it is your home. Nestle in. Enjoy your stay. I am glad you are here.

MI VIAJE ES TU VIAJE

"Mi viaje es tu viaje" is the experience I hope you had when you read this book. "My journey is your journey." That's what I want you to take away from this experience. We are on this journey together.

The journey you take to discovering your Inner Samurai is the journey all women take. Although we may begin our journey from different starting points, eventually we all end up at the same place — at that place deep within, the place of our inner knower. Women know this place intuitively. This is the place of our inner strength. The repository of all our life experiences, alchemized from lead into pure gold. The place of our Inner Samurai.

As you discovered while reading this book, starting up a business is a journey. A journey to the heart of the inner woman. To her place of absolute knowing and personal power. To her Inner Samurai. To the seat of her wisdom and inner strength. To her place of extraordinary uniqueness and beauty.

This is the place where success is born, where success lives, and where success thrives. The more successful you are at tapping into your Inner Samurai, the more satisfying and successful a business you will have.

WHAT UNITES US ALL

The journey to discovering our Inner Samurai is the connective thread that unites us all. We have learned much through our journey together.

We have learned that there is a great and powerful force acting on our behalf, even if what we want for ourselves has not yet manifested. We have learned that everything is unfolding exactly as it is meant to be. While most new beginnings come at the end of some crash-and-burn experience, ultimately, the endings have been for our highest good and greatest well-being.

Who could forget Rosemary who thought she wanted to be a relationship coach and ended up teaching other women how to flip houses instead? And how about Helena who thought she would start up her business as a piano tuner only to end up as a music critic getting the best seats in the house wherever she goes?

Along our journey together, we learned that every perceived tragedy is a gift in disguise. Being downsized, outsourced, or fired from your corporate job might just be the very thing you need to propel you into the next great manifestation of your life.

Remember Victoria who was an industrial engineer by day and a closet milliner by night? Being downsized was exactly the impetus she needed to turn her passion into a sizeable profit and discover her true calling in the process.

How about Chrissie? She was so completely changed by the transformational experience of starting up a business that she completely changed her focus from helping moms stay at home with their newborns to becoming a wine and food tour guide in Italy!

Then, of course, there was Doris. Her story was one of the most amazing of all. Scammed by the man she loved, Doris not only recovered, but also became the owner of her own successful real estate business.

Through their experiences, we have learned that there are no accidents — only accidents by design. Synchronistic events, chance encounters, and coincidences are stepping-stones along our path leading us to something more, something greater.

Carrie was the perfect example of someone who followed one synchronistic event after another until she ended up sitting across from the woman who would become her new business attorney. Along the way, she discovered the importance of following every inner pulse, regardless if it made sense to her or not.

We have learned that it is never too late to quit, never too late to start. Never too late to pursue our dream, do what we want to do, or become who we want to be. Though some things will cease to be, other, better things will come into being. We have only to think our thoughts, and then align those thoughts with our Inner Samurai to bring them into manifestation.

Remember Sophie, the would-be chocolatier, who gave up too soon on her dream because of fear? Then there was Sarah. She hit her $250,000 goal because she had the courage to learn how to take inspired action, Inner Samurai style.

The Secret to Your Business Success

Each of the people and events you read about in this book had three things in common. You recognized them in the stories I told and the quotations I shared. Each time your heart was moved and passion stirred, you knew. Every time you found yourself engaged in someone else's journey, you knew. Whenever you opened to a new concept, thought, or way of looking at things, you knew, on some level, what I'm about to share with you.

As I bring this book to a close, I'd like to remind you of and leave you with three things. They are the secret to your business success. They are the essence of building a business from the inside out. They are the journey. Your business success rests on these three ingredients:

- The importance of knowing who you are.
- The value of accepting yourself as you are.
- The significance of daring to be who you are.

It's all about you, baby!

Knowing Who You Are

Your Inner Samurai will not let you forget who you are — a unique portion of God's essence, as contemporary author and speaker Wayne Dyer says. Because of this, your Inner Samurai will never lead you astray, will never steer you wrong, and is with you through thick and thin. And don't you forget it!

Discovering Your Inner Samurai:
The Entrepreneurial Woman's Journey to Business Success

Your Inner Samurai has always been with you, will always be with you, and is your constant partner and trusted advisor. Even if you decide to listen to the chattering voice inside your head, instead of your wise inner knower, your Inner Samurai is still there.

In the journey from Accidental Pren-her to entrepreneurial woman, many women are plagued by the question, "But what do I have to offer?" As my good friend, clinical psychologist Susan Olson, puts it so well in her foreword to this book: "I've seen women struggle with fears and doubts that have kept them from exploring their potentials and living their dreams." This is because so many women look outside themselves for the answers to questions that are best answered from within.

It's one thing to seek outside guidance and advice when writing your business plan, putting together your website, or learning about the latest recording technology for that podcast you want to do. It's quite another to seek outside advice on the important inner issue of knowing who you are and what you have to offer to the world.

Knowing who you are and what you have within are paramount to your business success. You have something unique to give the world that is yours and yours alone to give. Knowing what that unique thing is (or set of things are) will be what permeates your entire business. From customer relations to product development, from marketing strategy to how you run your business, this unique factor will be what infuses your entire business success.

One of my favorite stories that illustrates this point is *The Wise Woman's Stone.*

> A wise woman who was traveling in the mountains found a precious stone in a stream. Admiring it for its beauty, she picked it up and put it into her bag. The next day she met a fellow traveler who was hungry. She opened her bag to share her food, and when she did, the hungry traveler saw the precious stone and asked the woman to give it to him. She did so without hesitation. After they ate together, the traveler left, rejoicing in his good fortune. He knew the stone was precious and worth a lot of money . . . enough to give him shelter and feed him for life. But a few days later he came back to return the stone to the wise woman.
>
> "I've been thinking," he said, "I know how valuable the stone is, but I give it back in the hope that you can give me something even more precious. Show me what you have within you that enabled you to give me the stone."[1]

That which enabled the wise woman to give her fellow traveler the stone was her unique gift to the world. It wasn't the stone — the hungry man recognized that soon enough. It was something she had that was far greater than the stone.

What do *you* have within yourself? What is the unique, exclusive, exceptional gift that you have to offer? What rare or uncommon part of you needs to be expressed at this time in the world? What will keep your clients and customers coming back to you and asking for more, like the hungry man bringing back the stone to the wise woman? Whatever it is, that is your unique signature. The essense of who you are. This is the first ingredient of your business success.

Accepting Yourself As You Are

Along our journey together, you have been reminded of how unique and wonderful you are. You have a voice within that others are ready to hear, a touch others are ready to feel, a special way of looking at things that will open the eyes of another, and a particular way of perceiving things that will bring about illumination. You have a distinctive contribution to make to your community, your society, and to your world. No matter if it is to one person or to many, it is still yours to share, yours to give, and yours to accept.

Accepting that you can make a difference in the world is an extraordinary viewpoint. It's extra-ordinary because it goes beyond the ordinary way that most people view themselves. First, though, before you can accept that you have something extraordinary to give to the world, you must accept yourself as you are.

Remember Tina, the Certified Feng Shui Practitioner who was also interested in Ikebana and architectural design? She was full of good ideas, passionate about so much, and driving her boyfriend nuts, flitting from one thing to the next. Remember, too, how easily she was deflated when her boyfriend threw his hands in the air and said, "Can't you stick to one thing for awhile? Can't you just be normal?" Do you recall how hard it was for her to fit in? She thought there was something wrong with her until she accepted herself as a multiple-streams-of-passion person.

It was really tough on Tina. Has it been tough on you, too? It's tough on many of us. Have you found it difficult to fit in, blend in, or be "normal?" Well, who wants to be normal? Who wants to be, as Webster's Dictionary states: "conforming to the standard or the common type; usual, regular?"[2] You are a unique portion of God's essence. That doesn't sound so "common" or "regular," does it? Get over trying to fit in. Get over trying to be normal. Instead, get on with being the unique and extra-ordinary woman that you are.

Accepting who you are is what Miyamoto Musashi's first rule is all about. This rule states, "Do not think dishonestly."[3] It means being honest about you are. It's about accepting everything about yourself as distinctive, matchless, and irreplaceable.

This is the second ingredient to your business success. Accepting that you *are* distinct. That you *are* refreshingly one-of-a-kind. Accepting that you *are* rare and precious will change the way you view yourself and the contribution you have to make to the world. Accepting the idiosyncrasies, peculiarities, quirks and foibles that make you distinctively you. In fact, they will be the very things that will shape your appreciation of and for yourself.

Each one of us is different. Not one of us is normal. That's the beauty of who we are. Accept yourself. Then prepare to make an extra-ordinary difference in the world.

Dare to be Who You Are

Making an extra-ordinary difference in the world means daring to be who you are. This is a difficult thing for many women to do. In fact, it's a place where only a few women go. This third ingredient to success is often the most difficult one for women to express in the world, although it's the most natural direction to take once you know who you are and accept yourself as you are.

Daring to be who you are is to be someone. As clinical psychologist Susan Olson quotes French fashion designer Coco Chanel as saying, "How many cares one loses when one decides not to be something, but to be someone."

Daring to be who you are means embracing and living life. American mythology expert Joseph Campbell said, "We must be willing to get rid of the life we've planned, so as to have the life that is waiting for us."

And who could forget Ambrose Hollingworth Redmoon? A paraplegic confined to a wheelchair, he dared to pick up a pen and write, "Courage is not the absence of fear, but rather the judgment that something else is more important than one's fear."

Dare to be who you are. Not how someone else wants you to be. Be you. Now. Be the grandest version of the greatest vision you have about yourself right now. In the words of 19th century Dutch painter Vincent van Gogh, "One must work and dare if one really wants to live."

American actress Drew Barrymore, who has been through her share of ups and downs, knows risk. She has risked her reputation, her career, her fortune, and her life. In the end, though, she has come out the other side sure of herself and fully knowing who she is. "There's something liberating about not pretending. Dare to embarrass yourself. Risk," is her advice.

Looking back over her long life, African American poet Maya Angelou says, "I believe the most important single thing, beyond discipline and creativity, is daring to dare." According to American novelist Mary Sarton, "We have to dare to be ourselves, however frightening or strange that self may prove to be."

Dare to be who you are. What comes up for you when you read these words? Does some part of you, some part deep within, come to life, spark up, and take notice? Do you feel that quiet, sure inner voice pulse of *yes*? That's your Inner Samurai letting you know that daring to be who you are is what you were born to do — what your life purpose is all about.

Look no further. You *are* extra-ordinary. You do have something unique and special to offer the world. Dare to show it. Dare to offer it. The world is your oyster. The Universe is working on your behalf for all great and good things. Everything exists in your now. You are never alone. We are in this together. *Mi viaje es tu viaje.*

>Success is assured,
>
>Greatness is,
>
>Beauty surrounds, and
>
>All is well. [4]

I end this writing on August 19, 2007, with gratitude and joy for the journey.

Susan L. Reid, DMA
Massanutten, VA

ENTREPRENEURIAL WOMEN BUSINESS SUCCESS RESOURCES

LAUNCH YOU! e-Zine
Sign up to receive free, bi-weekly small business start-up and launch tips, ideas, and resources for entrepreneurial women via email. Subscribe at: www.alkamae.com

Alkamae Blog
Created with the Accidental Pren-her in mind, this blog is about sharing the journey of turning entrepreneurial women into successful small business owners, from the inside out — the Inner Samurai Way. Subscribe via RSS or e-mail so that you won't miss a single post at: www.susanreid.typepad.com

Discovering Your Inner Samurai **Tips and Tools**
Download and utilize a growing collection of tools, articles, and resources designed to help you implement the concepts and strategies discussed in each chapter of this book at: www.alkamae.com/articles.php

Small Business Start-up Coaching and Consulting
At Alkamae, we specialize in taking the fear out of starting up your business, so you can get on with the business of transforming lives and making a difference in the world. If you are interested in exploring this possibility together, email me at: Susan@SuccessfulSmallBizOwners.com

A Note from the Illustrator

The act of becoming; it is a present moment act. It is carved every second, with every fiber of your being.

— Lee Harris

Susan builds businesses by getting to the heart of the owner's desires and growing them into full form. I met her last year on a conference call and I knew immediately that we would work together.

The method Susan uses for extracting inner wisdom from her clients is to gently coax and inspire, until the truth is revealed. My truth was that it was important for me to build a business that was an extension of who I am. When I became frustrated with this project, Susan had me focus on my passions. When asked what makes my heart sing, I gave answers that had very little to do with what Susan and I were actually working on. In fact, I couldn't see how my love of energy, the Universe, and drawing related to each other in any sensible way.

Susan's coaching then took me on a tour of myself, helping me put the pieces together to form a whole that resonated deeply. A couple of weeks later, I had a strong inspiration to grab a pen and let it hit the paper any way it wanted to. In that moment, there was a strong connection between my heart and my pen, one that I hadn't experienced before. Everything began to make sense.

Two days later, I was asked if I'd consider illustrating this book. I was very excited! We talked about what Susan wanted and she sent me a chapter to read. Beginning with the word "Home," I set to work on an "H" because letters felt like a great container for my symbols, shapes, and lines. The moment I finished that "H," I was inspired to start another drawing. Out came the "T" that you see as the graphic on the cover of this book. As I moved my pen across the paper, the lines seemed to know exactly where to go, I just followed along. When I was done, I stared at my work, wondering where it had all come from.

Susan's reaction to my "T" was immediate and enthusiastic. She said she had been looking for a new Inner Samurai image and asked if she could use my "T" for that purpose. And that's the story behind how my "T" became Susan's Inner Samurai image on the front of her book. I believe that Susan called forth this symbol of her Inner Samurai through me. That's exactly the kind of energy exchange we've experienced all along. Co-creating with Susan is fun and enlightening, and with her guidance, I've discovered a deeper place within myself. From here, anything is possible. Thank you, Susan, for assisting me on my path.

Dana Weekley
Titusville, NJ

Notes

Preface

[1] Eccl. 3.1-8 KJV.

Chapter 1

[1] Ambrose Hollingworth Redmoon, "No Peaceful Warriors," *Gnosis: A Journal of the Western Inner Traditions* 21 (1991): 40-45.

[2] "Take This Sabbath Day," Season 1, Episode 14, *The West Wing*.

Chapter 2

[1] Wayne W. Dyer, *Inspiration: Your Ultimate Calling* (Carlsbad: California, 2006), 82.

Chapter 3

[1] Eckhart Tolle, *A New Earth* (New York: Dutton, 2005), 117-118.

Chapter 6

[1] Joseph Campbell, *The Hero with a Thousand Faces* (Princeton: Princeton University Press, 1949).

[2] Ibid.

[3] J.R.R. Tolkien, *The Fellowship of the Ring* (Boston: Houghton Mifflin, 2001), 81.

[4] The correct quotation is: "'Tis better to have loved and lost than never to have loved at all."

[5] Susan L. Reid's personal motto.

Chapter 7

[1] Webster's College Dictionary (1991), s.v. "Intuition."

[2] Shirley Bazar Steer, *Now I Know I'm Okay: A Typology Handbook on Relationships* (Bryan, TX: Insight Publishing, 1989), 21.

[3] Joe Vitale, *The Attraction Factor* (Hoboken: John Wiley and Sons, 2005), 45.

[4] Goddard Neville, *The Law and the Promise* (Carmarillo, CA: DeVorss Publications, 1961), 14.

Chapter 9

[1] T. Harv Eker, *Secrets of the Millionaire Mind* (New York: Harper Collins, 2005), 2.

Chapter 10

[1] Lev. 16.21-22 RSV.

Chapter 11

[1] John Donne, *Devotions Upon Emergent Occasions and Death's Dual: With the Life of Dr. John Donne* (Vintage Press, 1999), 102.

Chapter 12

[1] Collins Concise Dictionary Plus (1989), s.v. "Solitude."

[2] Omar Khayyam, *Rubaiyat of Omar Khayyam*, trans. Edward Fitzgerald (New York: Galahad Books, 1954), 155.

[3] Coach U is a leading global provider of coach training programs: http://www.coachinc.com/CoachU

[4] I first learned of this from my publisher at www.wmeblogs.com. They were early blog adopters of this method, and continue to blog professionally and teach others how to blog by using this method.

Chapter 14

[1] Unknown author.

[2] Webster's College Dictionary (1991), s.v. "Normal."

[3] Miyamoto Musashi, *The Book of Five Rings*, trans. Thomas Cleary (Boston: Shambhala, 2005), 21.

[4] Susan L. Reid's personal motto.

INDEX

A

Accepting yourself 270–271
Accidental Pren-her 10, 84, 90, 97, 98, 214, 236, 242, 247, 248, 268
  accident by design 2, 10
Accidental Pren-her™ xiii
Activating event 3, 4, 98, 275
Addams, Jane 83
Alkamae 3, 112, 277
Allowance 155–156
  hope floats on 155–156
  opposite reaction to resistance 156
Angelou, Maya 273

B

Baba Ram Dass 50
Barrymore, Drew 272
Bergman, Ingrid 119
Bernstein, Leonard 209
Blake, William xi
Blog 3, 214, 241, 242, 244, 277, 280
Blogging 241–244
Bolen, Jean Shinoda 141
Bootstrap 95
Borodin, Alexander 83
Buddha 19, 57, 58, 97
Burg, Bob 207

C

Campbell, Joseph 31, 97, 103, 272
Chanel, Coco vii, 272
Client examples
  Carrie 218–223, 259, 266
  Chrissie 111, 113, 265
  Doris 124–136, 266
  Freda 110
  Helena 106, 113, 265
  Kay 110
  Leslie 110
  Lola 120, 121
  Lori 108
  Rebecca 188–199
  Rita 234–244
  Rosemary 106, 112, 265
  Sarah 160–181, 266
  Tina 72–93, 108, 270, 271
  Victoria 248–259, 265
Confucius 58
Cooper, Rabbi David 210
2 Cor. 5:7 117
Courage, not absence of fear 13–14
Creative business plans 79

D

Daring to be who you are 271–273
Davidson, Robyn 9
da Vinci, Leonardo 82
Dillard, Annie 247, 258
Donne, John 223
Dooley, Mike 40
Duras, Marguerite 260
Dyer, Wayne 36, 157

E

Eastman, P. D. 37
Eco, Umberto 84
Effortless action 148, 149, 178
Einstein, Albert 118
Eker, T. Harv 170, 174
Emerson, Ralph Waldo 30
Energetic calendar 254–260
Entrepreneurial woman xi, 2, 6, 10, 97, 160, 268
Entrepreneurial women business success resources 276

F

Fear, action despite 13–14
Financial set point 170–174

G

Goals
  deliciousness of wanting more 160, 164
  emotional need flowing from incompleteness 166
  Maslow's Hierarchy of Needs 162–164
  need vs. want 162
  setting attainable 169–170
  success, clashing definitions 177
  the 60-40 Inner Samurai Rule 160
  the art of setting 159–184
  wants flowing toward abundance 166–167
God, meaning herein 19
God Self 5, 12
God Within 5, 12
Goethe, Johann Wolfgang von 83
Graham, Martha 71
Graves, Robert 118

H

Heroine's Journey 97–103, 105
Hildegard of Bingen 82
Hope
  floats on allowance 155–156
Hurnard, Hannah 103

I

Inner Samurai *passim*
  as effortless action 148
  energetic calendar 254–260
  inner knower 5, 12, 264, 268
  inner voice 4, 5, 11, 12, 109, 167, 273
    voice inside my head 5, 11, 13, 15, 33, 40, 46, 47
  priority and value systems 185–203
  pulse 6, 11, 13, 21, 47, 88, 120, 121, 122, 123, 124, 127, 132, 133, 137, 138, 217, 220, 221, 234, 245, 266, 273
  stress as your warning bell 179–180
  tapping into your 120–122
Inner Super Woman 5, 12
Intuition 117–124
  as Inner Samurai 119
  what intuition isn't 119–122

J

Jefferson, Thomas 83
Johnson, Spencer vii
Joyce, James 97

L

Lavater, Johann Kaspar 118
Lawrence, D. H. 138
Left-brain, right-brain, whole brain thinking 78–81
Leibniz, Gottfried 83

M

Magellan 129
Maslow, Abraham 49, 162
  Hierarchy of Needs 49, 162-164, 167
Maxwell, Elaine 114
Millionaire mindset 174
Mi viaje es tu viaje 264, 273

Index

Multiple-streams-of-passion 71, 72, 75, 77, 79, 80- 82, 84, 89, 90, 270
Musashi, Miyamoto 57
  The Book of Five Rings 57, 58, 59, 67, 281
    bodhisativa 57, 58, 61, 62, 67
    Guan Yin 57, 58, 61, 62, 67
    Kwannon 57, 58, 61, 62, 67
    nine rules 59–66

N

Networking 207–224
  the *Build the Relationship and They Will Come* game 219–224
Neville, Goddard 134
Newton, Isaac 155
Non-ego-based point of view 49, 54
Notes 279–281
Notes from Your Inner Samurai 30, 43, 54, 67, 93, 114, 138, 182, 204, 225, 245, 260

O

Observation mode 48
Olson, Susan ix, 268
Omega Center 210
Orman, Suze 204

P

Peyron, Pam 214
Planet and Moons game 85–89
Polymaths 81–91
Ptolemy, Claudius 82
Purkey, William W. 53
  Dance like there's nobody watching 53

R

Ram Dass 50, 53
Reality, what creates our 124–128
Redmoon, Ambrose Hollingworth 13–14, 272
Resistance 141–148
  fear is not 151–153
  scale of 1-10 154
  vs. allowance 154–155
  what resistance is 150–151
Rich, Adrienne 45
Riger, BZ 254
Roux, Joseph 227
Rowling, J.K. 95, 113
Rudolph, Wilma 43
Rumi 263

S

Sakharov, Andrei 83
Salk, Jonas 119
Sarton, Mary 273
Savant, Marilyn vos 115
Scapegoats
  history 187–188
  not about money, but value 200–203
  not about time, but priorities 188–199
  time and money 185–203
Scheduling chaos 247–259
Secret to business success 263–270
Selling 207–224
  the *Build the Relationship and They Will Come* game 219–224
Shakespeare, William 39
Shinn, Florence Scovel 54, 119
Sills, Beverly 93

285

Somerville, Mary 83
Soul 5, 12
Spirit 5, 12
Spiritual awakening, my 22–29
  roller coaster 45–46
Starting a business 103, 104
  a Heroine's Journey 103–105
  blogging 241–244
  five basic questions 105
    can I still have a life? 109–110
    do I have the education and experience? 110–112
    how do I obtain start-up money? 107–108
    idea good enough? 105–107
    what if I (don't) fail? 112–113
  isolation vs. solitude 227–244
  scheduling 247–259
  secret to business success 263–270
  vision statement 110–111
Steinem, Gloria 182, 185, 200
Stress
  your Inner Samurai's warning bell 179–180

T

Tao 57, 60, 61, 67, 90
Tennyson, Alfred Lord 112
The Fellowship of the Ring 100
The Hero's Journey: The World of Joseph Campbell 97, 114
The Hero with a Thousand Faces 97
The Tao of Pooh 67

The West Wing
  message from God episode 20–21
The Wise Woman's Stone 269
Thich Naht Hahn 22, 50
Tolle, Eckhart 32, 47–48, 159
Tyler, Liv 245
Tyndale, William 187

U

Unexpected, the xii

V

van Gogh, Vincent 272
Vitale, Joe 132
Voice inside our head 49, 51
Voice inside the head 61

W

Way 58, 59, 60, 61, 62, 67, 223, 277
  feminine 61
  non-action (vs. no action) 61
  non-action (vs. passive) 61
Wheatley, Margaret 225
Who am I now? 32–35
Who do you want to be now? 35
Winfrey, Oprah 75
Womaning
  woman as a verb 210–213

Z

Zen 57, 59, 211, 212

Gift?

Reading group?

Teaching material?

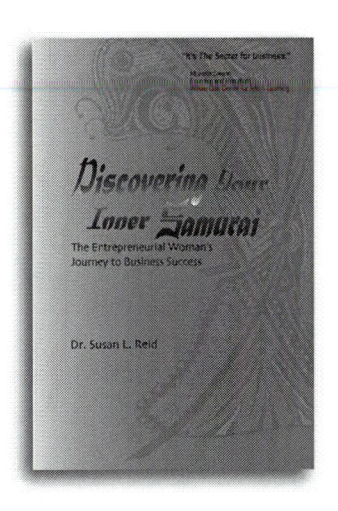

Order more copies of
Discovering Your Inner Samurai
online at:

    www.WMEBooks.com

Or call us toll-free:

    1-877-947-BOOK (2665)

Discounts available for education, special programs, and case quantities – give us a call.